Greece & Rome

NEW SURVEYS IN THE CLASSICS No. 25

GREEK THOUGHT

BY

CHRISTOPHER GILL

Published for the Classical Association

OXFORD UNIVERSITY PRESS

1995

Oxford University Press, Walton Street, Oxford OX2 6DP
Oxford New York Toronto
Delhi Bombay Calcutta Madras Karachi
Petaling Jaya Singapore Hong Kong Tokyo
Nairobi Dar es Salaam Cape Town
Melbourne Auckland
and associated companies in
Berlin Ibadan

ISSN 0017–3835
ISBN 019 922074–3

Printed in Great Britain
by Bell and Bain Ltd.,
Glasgow

PREFACE

This book explores four themes in the area of Greek thought, relating to psychology, ethics, politics, and the idea of nature as an ethical norm. As well as discussing important theories in Greek philosophy, I also discuss connections between Greek poetic and philosophical thinking. The issues raised by these themes and the basis for this selection of themes are explained in the Introduction. The book as a whole is designed to be a personal exploration of current scholarly work on Greek thought, which may be of interest to those who are not specialists in ancient philosophy as well as those who are.

I am grateful to the Editors of *Greece & Rome*, Peter Walcot and Ian McAuslan, for inviting me to contribute to this series on the subject of Greek thought, and for leaving me free how to interpret this interesting project. I am also grateful to Ian McAuslan for his patience and guidance in the editorial process. I would like to thank Richard Seaford for making time to comment helpfully on the book while it was being written. I am indebted also to successive generations of students, both at Aberystwyth and Exeter, with whom I have discussed many of the questions treated in this book; and I hope that it proves useful to future generations of such students and their teachers.

University of Exeter, June 1995   Christopher Gill

CONTENTS

NOTE ON CONVENTIONS

Greek works are cited by full title at first mention, and then by the standard short title, normally that listed in Liddell-Scott-Jones, *Greek–English Lexicon*. Unless otherwise indicated, references and quotations are based on the latest Oxford Classical Text. Secondary works are cited in the endnotes in full form at first mention, and then by short title; works cited in more than one chapter are given in full form at their first mention in each chapter, though subtitles are normally given only once. References to other parts of the book are given in this form: 'see Ch. II, text to nn. 79–83' or (within the same chapter) 'see text to nn. 79–83 below'. The following abbreviations are used:

AGP   *Archiv für Geschichte der Philosophie*
CQ   *Classical Quarterly*
HGP   W. K. C. Guthrie, *A History of Greek Philosophy*, 6 vols. (Cambridge, 1962–81); relevant vol. cited.
JHS   *Journal of Hellenic Studies*
LS   A. A. Long and D. N. Sedley, *The Hellenistic Philosophers*, 2 vols. (Cambridge, 1987); numbers cited refer to sections unless otherwise indicated.
OSAP   *Oxford Studies in Ancient Philosophy*
TAPA   *Transactions of the American Philological Association*

I. INTRODUCTION

The subject of 'Greek thought' is a potentially huge one, especially if one sets out to explore points of connection between Greek philosophy and thought in other areas of Greek culture, as I have done here. Rather than seek to provide a generalized picture of the whole subject, I have chosen to focus on four interconnected topics. These topics relate to Greek thinking about psychology, ethics, politics, and the connection between ethics and the study of nature. I have chosen these topics because they are ones on which I feel reasonably competent to outline recent developments, and on which I have some points of my own to make.[1] Also, these topics are some (but by no means all) of those that may be of particular interest to readers who are not specialists in ancient philosophy. This leaves scope for future possible surveys to cover subjects such as Greek medicine, science, and cosmology, as well as other central areas of Greek philosophy such as the theory of knowledge and metaphysics, which I do not discuss here. Within Greek philosophy, I consider, in varying degrees of detail, the Presocratics, the sophists and Socrates, Plato and Aristotle, the Stoics and Epicureans. Among other aims, I want to give some idea of the exciting new work, both exegetical and interpretative, being done on Hellenistic philosophy.[2] The decision to organize the book around themes and issues rather than thinkers or periods means that certain theories (such as that of Plato's *Republic*) are discussed several times from different standpoints.[3] However, this arrangement has the advantage of isolating and exploring certain issues in sufficient depth to bring out their interest and importance for contemporary scholarship. It also makes it possible to highlight certain significant parallels with intellectual issues that arise in other areas of Greek culture, notably Homeric epic and tragedy.

My first theme (Chapter II) is that of Greek ideas about character, personality, and the self. I discuss both the developmental approach taken in some well-known studies (especially those of Snell, Adkins, Dodds) and the approach of some scholars who stress, by contrast, certain key recurrent and continuing features in Greek thinking on human psychology. These features include the tendency to conceive the personality as a complex of interconnected parts rather than as centred on a unitary, self-conscious 'I'. They also include the presentation of rationality (rather than self-consciousness, subjectivity, or will) as the distinctively human characteristic. A further feature of Greek thought is that the understanding of the relationship between psychological parts (for instance, the management of emotions by reason) is linked with interpersonal and communal relationships and with shared debate about norms. I illustrate the model of personality involved by reference to, for instance, Homeric deliberative monologues, the great monologue in Euripides' *Medea*, the tripartite psyche in Plato's *Republic*, and the Stoic theory of the passions. I refer especially to recent scholarship (for instance, by Williams and Wilkes) which interprets Greek psychology in the light of some current psychological theories rather than of the seventeenth-eighteenth century models of personality (those of Descartes and Kant) assumed by developmental accounts such as those of Snell and Adkins.

My second theme (Chapter III) is that of ethics and values; I have two general aims in this chapter. One is to explore links between the dominant ethical values of Greek culture and those found in Greek philosophy. As in the case of Greek psychology, I discuss developmental approaches (especially those centred on the idea that there is a change from shame-culture to guilt-culture within the history of Greek ethical thought), and also outline criticisms of these approaches. Referring especially to recent work by Cairns, Williams, and others, I suggest that the idea of the *internalization* of ethical attitudes and ideas is important in Greek culture from Homer onwards, and (in this chapter and later ones) that this idea retains a significant role in the theories of Plato, Aristotle, and the Stoics. However, as I also bring out, this idea is combined with the belief that human beings can properly engage in debate about the nature and basis of the attitudes which should be internalized in their community.

A second aim in this chapter is to highlight the general tendency in recent scholarship on ancient philosophy to give a broadly positive account of the moral content and character of Greek ethical thought. This is in marked contrast with some earlier scholars (notably Prichard) who presented Greek ethical thought as deficient in its understanding of key moral ideas such as duty and altruism. The current tendency is shared both by scholars who see Greek ethical thought as relatively close to modern moral thinking of, for instance, a Kantian or Utilitarian type and by those (especially Williams and MacIntyre) who see Greek ethics as valuable precisely because it is different from much modern moral thought. This tendency has been especially marked in scholarship on Greek thinking about friendship, love, and other-benefiting virtue. Scholars have argued that the standard assumption of Greek philosophers that happiness is the overall goal of a human life is combined with the recognition that other people have strong ethical claims on us.

The two themes of this chapter converge on one issue. Recent scholars, by contrast with some earlier ones, have been ready to see Greek ethical theories as giving a positive value to altruism. I suggest that the Greek ideal of interpersonal life may be better understood as that of shared or mutual benefit, an idea which is linked, in turn, with that of the 'shared life' of family and close friendship or with that of reciprocity. This point may be particularly relevant to the ethical questions that arise in Plato and Aristotle about the competing claims of practical and contemplative wisdom to count as the highest form of human happiness.

The theme of the next chapter is, broadly, political theory; more specifically, Greek thinking about the relationship between the individual and the community. I stress that Greek thinking is not informed by the dominant modern contrast between the 'individual' (taken in isolation as a basic unit) and 'society' (in a large, generalized sense), or by the related political ideals of individualism and socialism. Greek political thinking (both in theoretical and non-theoretical contexts) presents human beings as naturally adapted to shape their lives by participation in one or more of a series of relationship-groups, such as the *oikos*, friendship-bond (this may include the philosophical 'school'), and *polis*. Such participation is typically conceived as making up a network of mutually beneficial relationships (a theme stressed in the preceding chapter) rather than being defined in terms of duties and obligations or rights, which are the dominant modern moral categories dealing with social relationships.

The idea that individuals have an inherent right to opt out of social relationships or to define their own private ethic is not, I suggest, normally part of Greek thinking. What takes its place is the thought that human beings, working together or on their own, properly examine the nature and basis of the types of community in which they are, or should be, engaged. I think that this point can help us to make sense of the apparently inconsistent stance of Socrates towards his community (as presented in Plato's *Apology* and *Crito*, for instance), as well as of Stoic and, to some extent, Epicurean thinking about communal life. I also stress that, although Greek philosophers are sometimes bitterly critical of the way of life practised in *particular types of* community (including their own) – Plato's *Republic* is an obvious example – they do not deny that human life is lived, in fact and ideally, in *communities*. I refer to recent work on Greek political theory from Socrates to Hellenistic philosophy as well as, in a more general way, post-war debate about Greek political thought since Popper.

The question whether 'nature' (either that of the universe as a whole or that of human beings as a natural kind) can serve as a norm for guiding

ethical or political life is one that figures in Greek philosophy from the Presocratics onwards. This question is partly analogous to that raised in Greek
poetry, especially Homer and tragedy, about whether the gods constitute
ethical norms for human life. It also relates to other well-marked features
of Greek intellectual life, such as the fifth-century debate about the relationship between *nomos* and *phusis* (roughly, 'ethics' and 'nature') and
popular criticism of intellectuals for impiety. The significance of the idea of
nature as a norm has figured prominently in some recent scholarship on
Greek philosophy, notably in connection with Aristotle and the Stoics. The
debate has been influenced by modern philosophical thinking about the
validity, or otherwise, of looking for moral norms in nature. In exploring
Greek thought on this question (Chapter V), I stress two points in
particular. One is the importance of attending closely to the kind of norms
supposedly validated in Greek thought by reference to the natural order or
kosmos, and of distinguishing these from those validated in this way in
Christian thinking, for instance. The other is the idea that development in
ethical character and development in understanding the ethical significance of the natural world go hand in hand, and cannot proceed properly
without each other. I think that attention to these points can help to show
that Greek thought on this subject is more complex, and perhaps more
credible to modern thinkers, than it might otherwise seem.

In my conclusion (Chapter VI), I draw out some common threads in the
four themes examined. Without imposing a specious unity on the thinking
of a complex culture from Homer to Hellenistic philosophy, I suggest that
Greek thought on these questions centres on the idea of a human being as
someone whose psychological, ethical, and political life is naturally shaped
by a nexus of interpersonal and communal relationships. I also suggest that
intellectual life (both inside and outside philosophical groups) is conceived
as an extension of this process, that is, as shared debate about common
truths.

NOTES

1. In the first two chapters, especially, I draw on ideas developed in a forthcoming book on Greek
psychology and ethics, *Personality in Greek Epic, Tragedy, and Philosophy: The Self in Dialogue*
(Oxford, 1996). These ideas are presented here in general terms, and located in the context of scholarly
debate on the relevant questions. See also Ch. VI, text to nn. 6–12.
2. For further reading on Greek philosophy, including some on areas not covered here, see the
Bibliographical Note (pp. 94–7 below).
3. The index enables readers to locate and amalgamate the points made on a specific theory or text.

II. MODELS OF THE SELF

The notion of the 'self', together with related ideas such as 'personality', 'character', can be used primarily in connection with human psychology, or ethical and social relationships, or a combination of these. In this chapter, I focus on the self as a psychological notion, taking up in Chapters III and IV related questions about ethical character and about the individual and society. On this topic, as on ethics and values, much recent debate has centred on the question whether we can trace a clear line of development within Greek culture, and on the related question of the relationship between Greek and modern conceptions of the self and the mind.

1. *Homeric and Tragic Psychology*

Much of this debate has taken its starting-point from two well-marked features of psychological language in Greek poetry. One is the fact that, in Homer and in subsequent Greek poetry, especially lyric and tragedy, psychological life is described in terms of the interplay between a complex of 'parts' or agents, including *thumos* ('spirit'), *menos* ('energy', 'excitement'), *kēr* ('heart') as well as *phrenes* ('thoughts', 'mind') and, to some extent, *psuchē* ('soul', 'life-force', as well as, sometimes, 'emotions'). The other is that, in Homer and, even more, in lyric and tragedy, human beings are sometimes presented, by themselves or others, as acting under the influence of an external or quasi-external force such as *atē* ('delusion'), madness (typically of a short, localized type), or divine intervention.

One type of response to these features has been to explain them by reference to the development of Greek ideas about the human mind and agency. Bruno Snell, for instance, claimed that both features, as present in Homer, indicate a relatively primitive understanding of human agency. In lyric, the stress on psychological passiveness indicates that human beings are at least beginning to be *conscious* of this deficiency. It is not before fifth-century tragedy, however, that we find human beings presented as conscious of their own capacity to make decisions. We also find, particularly in the great monologue in Euripides' *Medea* (1021–80, especially 1078–80), consciousness of division between 'reason' and the *thumos*. The fact that the division is seen as occurring *within the self*, rather than between the self and some 'external' force, is taken by Snell to show a nascent awareness of

psychological unity and agency, which was developed further in subsequent Greek philosophical thinking about the *psuchē*.[1]

Although other scholars have not necessarily seen the development as
taking place in quite this way, several well-known developmental accounts
have been offered since Snell's work. E. R. Dodds, for instance, associated
the role of *atē* ('delusion') in Homer with the influence of a 'shame-
culture'. Acts, such as Agamemnon's seizure of Achilles' prize-bride, which
proved to be mistaken and were a source of public 'shame', were external-
ized by being 'projected' on to a quasi-divine power.[2] A. W. H. Adkins,
analogously, associated the deficient understanding of human agency and
responsibility in early Greek poetry with a type of society in which people
are judged by reference to actions and the success and failure of those
actions, rather than by their conscious or deliberate intentions.[3] In the work
of J.-P. Vernant, a developmental pattern is combined with a structuralist
approach, in which poetic forms are seen as the expression of structures of
thought and society current at a particular time. The combination of
psychological agency and passivity in Greek tragedy (for instance, in the
presentation of Agamemnon's state of mind before sacrificing Iphigeneia,
in Aeschylus' *Agamemnon* 205–27) is seen as the expression of a particular
'historical moment'. The moment is one in which the institutions of citizen-
ship were replacing a framework of responsibility centred on the *oikos*,
'family' or 'household'. This change promoted a greater sense of one's
liability as an individual citizen, a sense which Aristotle later codified in his
analysis of the ideas of voluntariness and responsibility. Tragedy represents
a transitional point, when an emergent sense of individual responsibility is
fused with the older outlook, in which responsibility for one's actions is
shared between oneself, the household, and those divine powers, such as
Furies or 'a curse on the house', which are associated with the household.[4]

Other studies of early Greek psychology, such as those by Jan Bremmer
or D. B. Claus,[5] have tended to assume a developmental framework without explicitly offering a pattern of historico-cultural explanation. Ruth
Padel's account of the psychology of Greek tragedy takes a different line.
Padel stresses, like Snell, the passiveness of tragic psychology, and its open-
ness to madness and divine powers, as well as its strongly physical understanding of psychological parts, such as *splangchna* ('guts'). But she sees
these features as constituting a distinctively tragic perspective rather than
as being the expression of a culturally determined stage of development in
psychological understanding.[6]

In an important study, which marks a break with much preceding work
on Greek ethics as well as psychology, Bernard Williams has challenged the

assumptions underlying most developmental accounts. He argues that Snell and Adkins, in particular, make some very specific assumptions about what should count as a fully developed model of human agency. Snell assumes that a decision can only count as a 'genuine personal' decision if it is conceived as being made by someone who is conscious of making the decision, and who regards himself as an 'I', a unified centre of self-consciousness and will. Both he and Adkins presuppose a 'volitionist' model of human agency, in which action is regarded as the result of conscious acts of will. They also assume that a fully developed model of human agency implies a specific (and very strong) conception of human freedom. It implies that human beings are free, at a fundamental level, to will, choose, and act as they like, and should be held responsible accordingly. These assumptions are based, Williams argues, on the ideas of certain influential seventeenth- and eighteenth-century philosophers, especially Descartes and Kant; and the validity of these ideas has been disputed by many contemporary thinkers, including Williams. He challenges scholars who accept this type of developmental account to recognize that they are making strong (and questionable) assumptions about what counts as a fully developed model of human agency and responsibility.[7]

Williams also argues that the picture of human psychology given in Homer and Greek tragedy expresses what we moderns can still recognize as a credible and profound understanding of human experience. It expresses a proper sense of the ethical implications of the fact that human beings are sometimes subject to the force of their own emotions, or to the power of moral claims which do not derive solely from their deliberate actions as individuals. In particular, Greek poetry (more than Greek philosophy) expresses the power of two related ideas which are central to Williams's own thinking: those of 'agent regret' and of 'moral luck'. ('Moral luck' is, I think, the more general category, of which 'agent regret' is an aspect.) The central thought associated with 'moral luck' is that the ethical quality of a person's actions is determined not just by the quality of the intentions underlying the actions, but also by their outcome, which is affected by factors falling outside the control of the agent. The idea associated with 'agent regret' is that human beings properly accept some degree of moral responsibility for actions which they perform but do not perform deliberately. For instance, Oedipus' response to his (unintended) crimes and Heracles' response to his (unintended) killing of his family, namely those of pollution and shame, are morally intelligible to modern readers as well as to the original Greek audience. In so far as the psychology, as well as ethics, of early Greek poetry expresses these ideas, it expresses a profound response to human experience, rather than a primitive picture of human agency and responsibility.[8] The thought that Greek tragedy (as well as some Greek philosophy) can be read as expressing these ideas has been explored especially by Martha Nussbaum in a wide-ranging study of Greek tragic and philosophical thinking.[9]

Whether or not we accept in full Williams's claims, they are very important, I think, because they cause us to raise fundamental questions about the assumptions we make in studying Greek psychological and ethical models. In reflecting on the implications of his views, it is helpful to take them together with some partly parallel claims made in connection with Greek philosophical accounts of human psychology. Kathleen Wilkes, for instance, points both to Homeric and to Aristotelian psychology as alternatives to what she sees as the misleading model of the human mind offered by Descartes, which is centred on a unitary 'I', a source of self-consciousness and will. This model, she argues, is based on false ideas about psychological unity and about the extent to which human psychological life takes place on the conscious level. The Homeric presentation of human psychological life as the interplay between a complex of parts or agents (*thumos*, *phrenes*, etc.) can be seen as, in this respect, more credible, and closer to the kind of model offered by, for instance, modern 'functionalist' psychology.[10] Functionalists, such as Daniel Dennett, analyse human action in terms of the interplay, or communication, between functions or systems, rather than in terms of conscious intentions. In Plato, Aristotle, and some other Greek accounts, human psychology is also pictured, as in Homer, as the interplay between parts or functions (for instance, between reason and 'spirit' or desire). The parallel with modern functionalist psychology, it is sometimes suggested, can help us to see the Greek philosophical, as well as poetic, versions of this model as intelligible and credible rather than as being defective because they are not sufficiently like Descartes's model.[11]

Another parallel that is sometimes drawn is that between modern 'action-theory', of the type advanced by Donald Davidson, and Aristotelian or Stoic analysis of human motivation. The key feature of Davidson's approach lies in explaining human action by reference to the beliefs and desires expressed in the action, whether or not the person acting is conscious of these as motives.[12] Scholars have seen Aristotle's use of the 'practical syllogism' (logical reasoning used to analyse motivation), as implying a similar approach. The stages of the syllogism express the beliefs and desires from which the action (as in a logical argument) 'follows', whether or not the person concerned is fully conscious of all these stages (sometimes she[13] is explicitly said not to be).[14] Similarly, in the Stoic model, the rational 'appearances' or 'impressions' (*phantasiai*), which express the way things 'look' to human beings, play a crucial role in explaining human action. The fact that people 'assent' (say yes) to certain types of impression, namely those that ascribe value to courses of action, is adequate to explain the 'impulse' (*hormē*) to act in a given way. These impressions and assents may or may not be conscious: but what explains the action is not the fact that the process is a conscious one (or that it involves a self-conscious 'I') but the fact that the action 'follows' from the beliefs underlying the impressions and assents.[15] Again, this forms a contrast with the pattern assumed by Snell and Adkins, for whom a fully developed psychological model is one in which actions are conceived as based on conscious volitions.

If we return to the interpretation of Homeric psychology with these later Greek and modern ideas in mind, the position seems very different rom the way it has seemed in most developmental accounts. The deliberative monologues found in battle-scenes in the *Iliad* can be seen as expressing an understanding of human motivation which resembles that found both in later Greek theories and in modern action-theory. The monologues express reasoning, either (1) in the form of working out the means to a given end, or (2) putting a given act in a general class. For instance, we find (1): 'if I do this, this will happen', or (2): 'this is the kind of thing a brave chieftain does, so I shall do this'.[16] The pattern can be seen as a version of Aristotle's account of deliberation. Alternatively, it can be sen as anticipating the Stoic model, in which human agents 'assent' to 'impressions' about what is worth doing. In Stoic terms, the stages of the monologues express the way the situations 'appear' to the people concerned; and they conclude by saying 'yes' (or 'no') to the possible courses of action presented in this way.[17] As so interpreted, these patterns of reasoning embody a valid model of motivation. The fact that they do not present self-conscious acts of will, in which the agent is conscious that *he* is choosing, does not make them any less adequate as representations of deliberation.

What about the more 'passive' side of Homeric and tragic psychology; has recent work provided any framework of explanation which is different from, or more useful than, that assumed by developmental accounts such as those of Snell and Adkins? I have already noted Williams's claim that this reflects, in part, a proper response to the recognition that, on some occasions, human beings are subject to forces within themselves, their situations, or the ethical claims that those situations bring (text to n. 8 above). Another line of explanation is to refer to the framework of social and interpersonal judgements that determine whether or not a given emotional response is presented as active or passive, as deriving from 'me' or from some psychological feature that is, in some sense, not 'me'. This line of explanation was adopted by Dodds in his explanation for the Homeric use of the idea of *atē* (as famously employed by Agamemenon in *Iliad* 19). This line of explanation can be developed, without necessarily adopting Dodds's associated ideas about 'shame-ethics'.[18]

For instance, if we look at the different forms of psychological language used by the speakers in *Iliad* 9, we can see a connection between their view of the rights and wrongs of the situation and their attempts to encourage Achilles to see himself as active or passive in relation to his anger, his *thumos* ('spirit'), *cholos* ('anger' or 'bile'), or *mēnis* ('wrath'). Generally, the speakers present Achilles as able to 'control' or 'suppress' his *thumos*, and offer him what they see as good reasons why he should do so.[19] But Phoenix also cites the counter-example of Meleager, as someone who maintained his anger unreasonably, and who gave it up without gaining advantage from doing so. He describes Meleager's psychological state in passive terms, saying that there 'came on him' the anger or bile (*cholos*) which can 'swell' even in the hearts of those who are generally sensible; and that, in giving his anger up with no gain to himself, his '*thumos* was aroused', and he 'gave way to his *thumos*' (9. 553–5, 595–8). Achilles himself, at a key moment in the scene, says that he sees the force of what is being said, but that 'his heart swells with anger' when he thinks how shamefully he has been treated (9. 645–8). This is often taken as indicating that Achilles accepts that he is in the wrong, and that he is, like Meleager (as presented by Phoenix), carried away by his feelings.[20] But it is more likely that, in this case, 'passive' psychological language is used in connection with an emotion that the speaker thinks it is right for him to feel, even if he sees that there are reasons (and feelings) pointing in another direction.[21]

A more striking, and much-examined, case is the great monologue in Euripides' *Medea* in which Medea nerves herself to carry out her plan of punishing her husband by killing their children. In the course of this speech, Medea identifies herself with, or distances herself from, this plan, and the part of herself that she sees as making her fulfil this plan (sometimes expressed as her *thumos*). At the close of the speech, she sees *thumos* (in the translation which I favour) as 'master of my [revenge] plans', and as making her perform an act that she herself sees as, in some ways, 'bad'. But at an earlier, and decisive, stage, she has identified herself with these plans and the associated feelings, and renewed her resolve not to 'weaken' the hand that will carry out the act.[22] Snell, as noted earlier, sees this speech as signifying a crucial stage in the development of the idea of the self, that in which Greek culture first expressed the idea of conflict *within the self* (text to n. 1 above). I have already outlined reasons why one might not accept Snell's account of the history of Greek psychology. I think that this case is more plausibly seen as a very striking example of a phenomenon that can be found both in earlier and later Greek thought. This is the use of psychological language of different kinds (including active and passive language, and self-identifying and self-distancing language) to express an ethical judgement on the stance being adopted.[23]

The determining factor in such cases, I think, is not just the speaker's individual or subjective feeling at any one time, but rather what she thinks that it is right or 'reasonable' to feel and do, given the situation and its ethical claims. In other words, psychological language, in Greek epic and tragedy, can be seen as part of the 'argument' which the figures have about the rights and wrong of courses of action, as well as being part of the 'argument' that the play or epic as a whole constructs.[24] One idea that can be deployed usefully in this connection is that acts such as Medea's infanticide are seen by the person doing them as 'exemplary gestures', designed to dramatize exceptional wrongdoing, such as Jason's betrayal of his wife's exceptional benefits to him. Although these acts are, as is acknowledged by the person concerned, wrong by conventional standards, they are seen by them as justifiable ways of dramatizing the nature of the wrongs they have suffered. Although Medea's infanticide, and the feelings that motivate it, are, by conventional standards, wholly 'unreasonable', from Medea's standpoint (and on the basis of her implied 'reasoning' about the ethics of the situation), it is justified as an exemplary gesture.[25]

2. *Greek Philosophical Psychology*

A broadly similar type of interpretation can be applied to the presentation of normative and defective psychological states in Greek philosophy. As noted earlier, recent scholarship has tended to interpret this material in the light of current theories of mind, such as functionalism or action-theory, rather than the earlier modern theories (those of Descartes or Kant) assumed by Snell and Adkins. This change has led to a more positive treatment of the Greek tendency to present human psychological life in the form of the interplay between parts and functions (which Snell and Adkins saw as the mark of a primitive understanding of the personality). It has also led to greater interest in the idea that human emotions and desires are, characteristically, shaped by beliefs and reasoning. These developments have been particularly marked in scholarly treatments of Aristotle's account of *akrasia* (usually translated as 'weakness of will') and of related Greek theories of psychological interplay and conflict.[26]

A theory that has aroused renewed interest in this connection is Plato's tripartite model of the *psuchē* in the *Republic*. This has sometimes been seen as a rather implausible psychological model; in particular, the 'spirited' (*thumoeides*) part has been regarded as an artificial element, supplied as an equivalent for the 'auxiliary' class in the ideal state. However, it can be seen as an intelligible continuation of the role of *thumos* in earlier Greek psychology, and as developing the ethical role of shame and honour associated with this element in Greek poetry. Also, central to Plato's concerns in the *Republic* is the question of the extent to which the personality as a whole (including emotional aspirations and, to some extent, desires) can be shaped by ethical ideals; and the spirited part plays a key role in this respect.[27] The presentation of psychological life as the interplay or dialogue between parts or functions in the *Republic* and *Phaedrus* has been compared with Dennett's functionalist model or that of Freud.[28] The comparison with Freud is especially suggestive because Freud is also interested in the idea that the nature of the interplay between the parts of the personality is shaped by success or failure in development (a development that Freud analyses in psycho-sexual as well as psycho-social terms). However, a difference that needs to be underlined is that for Freud the parts are defined by reference to what does or does not constitute the self-conscious 'I' (the *ego* or *Ich*), whereas for Plato and other Greek thinkers the key agent is 'reason' rather than the self-conscious 'I'.

In considering the role of reason in Greek ethical psychology, it is important to see that the term 'reason' (*logos*) conveys three main types of meaning. It can signify a certain type of function (such as reasoning, judging, or knowing). It can signify a norm: that is, the 'right' or 'reasonable' way to act, feel, or think. It can also signify a mode of desire, namely the desire to fulfil the best possible function of reason, however this is conceived. Although Greek thinkers such as Plato tend not to distinguish these senses explicitly, we need to do so to understand their theories. In the *Republic*, for instance, the ideal of 'reason's rule' does not only signify a psychic state in which rational functions 'rule' aspirations and desires (which have also, in some sense, been 'persuaded' to be ruled in this way).[29] It also signifies a state in which the rational and other functions are shaped by *right* (reasonable) ideals. Further, the best possible human state, one which may not be within reach of many people, is that of being 'ruled' by the best possible human desire, namely that of knowing, and living in the light of, objective ethical truth, or the Form of the Good. As the *Republic* stresses, the effect of the latter kind of rule is to reshape aspirations and desires in a way that can enable reason-ruled philosophers to be self-controlled (*sōphrōn*) and brave in a more complete way even than ordinarily virtuous people.[30] This makes them peculiarly well-equipped to set psychological and ethical standards for other people. However, as Plato acknowledges, it may also make them more strongly inclined to pursue truth through philosophical enquiry than to play their ethico-political role (though they will also be ready to play this role).[31]

In Plato's theory, as in Medea's monologue and other poetic passages, the question of what counts as right or 'reasonable' is crucial in determining the presentation of the nature and interrelationship of the psychological parts. The same general point can be made about Aristotle's analysis of *akrasia* in *Nicomachean Ethics* (*NE*) 7. 3. *Akrasia* is sometimes translated as 'weakness of will', and this term can suggest, misleadingly, an unsuccessful contest between rational will and wholly non-rational desire or passion (this is a Kantian model, and one that seems to be in Snell's mind in his account of the *Medea*).[32] However, this model does not fit Aristotle's account of *akrasia*, which is analysed (through the practical syllogism) in terms of two competing lines of reasoning, justifying two contrasting courses of action.[33] What is it that determines which of these two lines of reasoning is successfully carried through and put into action? In particular, why is it the line of reasoning that the person concerned would *not* normally approve that is put into action? The explanation seems to be that the (correct) ethical beliefs of the person concerned have not, through ethical education and development, become fully integrated into her character or 'nature'. Although Aristotle at one point describes the akratic process as the result of 'desire' (or 'appetite', *epithumia*) disrupting the practical syllogism that would otherwise be carried through, it seems clear from his general analysis that this is not a contest between 'brute' desire and moral reason. Rather, it is a case where the belief-and-desire patterns that motivate action have not been *fully* brought into line, through character-development, with those which the person herself recognizes as the right (reasonable) ones.[34]

Although the interpretation of Aristotle's theory is (to a greater extent than I can indicate here) a matter of controversy, all recent accounts accept, I think, the general point that Aristotle's model presupposes that the operation of desire is amenable to analysis in terms of beliefs and reasoning, and that desire can be shaped by the development of character. In doing so, they reflect, if not always explicitly, some dominant modern ways of thinking about the belief-based character of emotion and about the influence of social norms on the formation of desire. Such thinking has also contributed to a reappraisal of the Stoic theory of the emotions or passions (*pathē*). This theory has sometimes been seen as an unrealistically 'rational-ist' or 'intellectualist' one (as has Socrates' theory in Plato's *Protagoras*);[35] but recent work can put it in a different perspective. In claiming that emotions *are* beliefs, Chrysippus, the main systematizer of Stoic theory, can be seen as accentuating the belief-based conception of emotions which is implied in other Greek theories, possibly including Plato's. More pre-cisely, Chrysippus claims that *pathē* are *false* beliefs, specifically, false beliefs about what is and is not valuable and worth pursuing. Further, they are beliefs that it is right to react in a given way. As noted earlier (text to n. 17 above), in Stoic theory, beliefs of this sort (expressed in the form of assent to rational impressions) are taken to be sufficient to trigger motivating responses. In the case of passions, the responses include certain intense affective psychophysical reactions: a 'shrinking before what is thought to be a thing to avoid' and a 'rising up at what is thought to be a thing to pursue'.[36] In this way, the Stoic theory gives a place for the affective and psychophysical dimension of emotions and desires; in this respect, the theory is not at all 'intellectualist'. But it combines this view of emotions with the claim that, in adult humans at least, beliefs (in the form of assent to impressions) are required to trigger these reactions.

The Stoics are generally supposed (like Socrates) not to accept that *akrasia* occurs: if affective reactions are thought to depend on beliefs, there seems to be no room for the idea that anyone could fail to act and feel in line with her beliefs. None the less, Chrysippus evidently showed great interest in the lines in Euripides' *Medea*, in which she articulates her state of psychic conflict (1078–80). More generally, he is interested in cases where people express at the time the fact that what they are doing is mis-guided, but still persist in doing it. One reason for this interest seems to be that Chrysippus thought that such people are themselves expressing a view of their state which corresponds with the Stoic conception of a passion. When Medea says, 'I know that what I am about to do is bad', she expresses the realization that her emotion is based on (what Chrysippus would see as) a *false* belief (that it is right to react with anger at Jason, and to want to take revenge on him in this way).[37] When Medea says (in the translation that Chrysippus assumes) 'but *thumos* is stronger than my deliberations',[38] she expresses the fact that a passion is an 'excessive impulse', which, though based on belief, can become out of control, like legs that are running rather than walking. Indeed, the fact that she recognizes the badness of what she is doing, but still persists in this, also bears out this feature of a passion.[39] Thus, Chrysippus, despite holding in the strongest possible form a belief-based model of emotion, combines this with an analysis of psychological conflict, and a recognition of the intense power of what are normally seen as purely affective reactions.[40]

The question whether Chrysippus' psychological model is credible or not was much debated in antiquity. It seems that one of his successors as head of the Stoic school, Posidonius, modified his theory, arguing that we need to recognize the existence of 'affective motions' (*pathētikai kinēseis*), even in adult humans, which are not based on beliefs and reasoning. Posidonius also went back, according to some accounts, to a model more like that of the tripartite *psuchē* in Plato.[41] However, the evidence for this debate within the Stoic school is largely based on the much later medical writer Galen, who is bitterly opposed to Chrysippus' theory, and may exaggerate the differences between the two Stoic theories.[42]

The debate about emotions in antiquity, and the pervasive Greek idea (found in the Epicurean and other schools as well as in Stoicism) that philosophy can serve as a mode of cure or 'therapy' for the emotions, has become a subject of great scholarly interest.[43] What is fuelling this interest is not just recent scholarly awareness of the relatively under-examined wealth of intellectual material in Hellenistic (and Roman) writings. Also important is the awareness, which I have highlighted in this chapter, that Greek and contemporary models of mind and psychology are now seen as much closer to each other than they were when the prevalent models were based on thinkers such as Descartes and Kant. Nor is this process simply one of the importation of modern ideas into the exegesis of ancient texts. In the current climate, it is being appreciated that, although Greek psychological thought can be illuminated by reference to modern thought, it also has valid insights to contribute to contemporary debate. It can be argued that the quality and penetration of Greek thought on psychological conflict, and on forms of therapy for emotions and desires, compare favourably with much contemporary psychological and psychotherapeutic thought. The exploration of the interplay between beliefs/reasoning and affective states, and of the preconditions and modes of therapy in, for instance, Stoic theory can stand comparison with contemporary cognitive or psychoanalytic theory and therapy.[44]

I have organized this chapter as, in large measure, a contrast between developmental accounts and those, such as Williams's, which emphasize the analogies between Greek and modern thought and the continued relevance of Greek ideas to contemporary debate. It is, of course, quite possible that developmental accounts of Greek psychology could be offered which would take account of these recent approaches. Such accounts might explain, as part of their project, the kind of connections between Greek and modern thinking that have been emphasized recently. But I think it is right to say that no such developmental accounts have yet been offered.

NOTES

1. B. Snell, *The Discovery of the Mind*, tr. R. G. Rosenmeyer (New York, 1960, based on the 2nd edn. of the German version, 1948), chs. 1, 3, and 6, esp. pp. 123–7; *Scenes from Greek Drama* (Berkeley, 1964), pp. 52–6.

2. See E. R. Dodds, *The Greeks and the Irrational* (Berkeley, 1951), ch. 1, esp. pp. 2–8, 13–18, discussing esp. *Iliad* (*Il.*) 19. 86–94.

3. A. W. H. Adkins, *From the Many to the One: A Study of Personality and Views of Human Nature in the Context of Ancient Greek Society, Values and Beliefs* (London, 1970), pp. 1–9, 24, 47, 90, 124, 126, 196–7, 271. His approach to psychology is linked with his approach to the history of moral ideas in his more famous study, *Merit and Responsibility: A Study of Greek Values* (Oxford, 1960), on which see Ch. III, text to n. 7.

4. J.-P. Vernant and P. Vidal-Naquet, *Tragedy and Myth in Ancient Greece*, tr. J. Lloyd (Brighton, 1981), chs. 2–3; for this type of approach, see also S. Saïd, *La Faute tragique* (Paris, 1978), part 2. For a non-developmental reading of the combination of psychologically active and passive language in such cases, see C. Gill, 'The Character-Personality Distinction', in C. B. R. Pelling, ed., *Characterization and Individuality in Greek Literature* (Oxford, 1990), pp. 1–30, esp. pp. 17–31.

5. J. Bremmer, *The Early Greek Concept of the Soul* (Princeton, 1983); D. B. Claus, *Toward the Soul: An Inquiry into the Meaning of Psyche Before Plato* (New Haven, 1981).

6. R. Padel, *In and Out of Mind: Greek Images of the Tragic Self* (Princeton, 1992); also *Whom Gods Destroy: Elements of Greek and Tragic Madness* (Princeton, 1995). Her stress on the physical character of the Greek conception of psychological organs and experiences recalls R. B. Onians, *The Origins of European Thought* (Cambridge, 1954, 2nd edn.). But, in her case, this stress is also informed by psycho-analytic and feminist approaches, as well as anthropological ones.

7. B. Williams, *Shame and Necessity* (Berkeley, 1993), chs. 1–3, esp. pp. 21–31, 40–2; for a more detailed analysis of the assumptions of Snell and Adkins, see C. Gill, *Personality in Greek Epic, Tragedy, and Philosophy: The Self in Dialogue* (Oxford, 1996), 1.1.

8. Williams, op. cit., pp. 68–74, and ch. 6, esp. pp. 133–9, 158–67. On the concepts of moral luck and agent regret, see Williams, *Moral Luck* (Cambridge, 1981), ch. 2, esp. p. 30 n. 2, suggesting the relevance of these concepts to Greek tragedy.

9. M. C. Nussbaum, *The Fragility of Goodness: Luck and Ethics in Greek Tragedy and Philosophy* (Cambridge, 1986), esp. chs. 1–3 and 13 (on tragedy); Nussbaum also sees these ideas as expressed in some Greek philosophy, esp. in Aristotle's thinking on happiness, and, in a complex and ambivalent way, in Plato's *Symposium* and *Phaedrus*; see her chs. 6–7, 11–12.

10. K. Wilkes, *Real People: Personal Identity without Thought Experiments* (Oxford, 1988), chs. 6–7.

11. For a functionalist model of mind, see D. Dennett, *Brainstorms: Philosophical Essays on Mind and Psychology* (Hassocks, Sussex, 1979), ch. 9; Dennett's approach is compared with that of Plato in the *Republic* (*R.*) by J. Annas, *An Introduction to Plato's Republic* (Oxford, 1981), pp. 142–6, 149–52. On the contrast between Cartesian and functionalist models of mind, see P. Smith and O. R. Jones, *The Philosophy of Mind: An Introduction* (Cambridge, 1986); connections between Aristotle's theory and functionalism are made in their pp. 75–83, 177–9, 254–9. See also C. Gill, 'Is there a Concept of Person in Greek Philosophy?', in S. Everson, ed., *Psychology: Companions to Ancient Thought 2* (Cambridge, 1991), 166–93, considering links between Aristotelian and Stoic conceptions of human rationality and some modern non-Cartesian theories about being a 'person' or 'rational animal'. On Greek theories and that of Freud (another critic of the Cartesian model) see text to n. 28 below.

12. D. Davidson, *Essays on Actions and Events* (Oxford, 1980), chs. 1–3; E. LePore and B. P. McLaughlin, edd., *Action and Events: Perspectives on the Philosophy of Donald Davidson* (Oxford, 1985), pp. 3–13.

13. In this book, I use 'he/she' or 'her/him' indifferently as indefinite personal pronouns, even when summarizing ancient authors who use only masculine forms for this purpose; however, when translating these authors, I retain their practice in this respect.

14. See e.g. Aristotle (Arist.), *De Motu Animalium* 701a17–28, in which 25–8 comments that not all stages of the practical syllogism are necessarily noticed by the mind. See further, on the relevance of theories such as Davidson's to the interpretation of Aristotle's psychological model, E. Anscombe, *Intention* (Oxford, 1957), p. 79; M. C. Nussbaum, *Aristotle's* De Motu Animalium (Princeton, 1978), pp. 165–220, esp. 165–6; D. Charles, *Aristotle's Philosophy of Action* (London, 1984), pp. 1–4; T. Irwin, *Aristotle's First Principles* (Oxford, 1988), ch. 15, nn. 3, 6, 9, on p. 596.

15. See B. Inwood, *Ethics and Human Action in Early Stoicism* (Oxford, 1985), ch. 3; J. Annas, *Hellenistic Philosophy of Mind* (Berkeley, 1992), ch. 4. On the linkage with modern non-Cartesian theories, see Gill, 'Is There a Concept of Person in Greek Philosophy?', pp. 184–93. A further possible parallel is between Stoic psychology and modern theories centred on the idea that mental states should be analysed in terms of their 'content', or what they 'represent', regardless of whether these states are conscious or not; see R. Sorabji, 'Perceptual Content in the Stoics', *Phronesis* 35 (1990), 307–14, at p. 308 n. 5.

16. The 'if I do this, this will happen' pattern is found in all four deliberative monologues in the *Iliad*: see 11. 404–6, 17. 91–6, 102–5, 21. 553–70, 22. 99–130. The second pattern is clearest in 11. 408–10; see also 17. 98–9. For the claim that the Homeric monologues represent valid (though non-Cartesian) modes of deliberation, see R. Gaskin, 'Do Homeric Heroes Make Real Decisions?', *CQ* NS 40 (1990), 1–15, Williams, *Shame and Necessity*, ch. 2.

17. The formulaic line, 'But why does my spirit debate this with me?' (which occurs in all four Iliadic monologues), can be taken as indicating the moment at which the Homeric figure 'says no' to an 'impression' about what is worth doing in a given situation. On these parallels between Homeric, Aristotelian, and Stoic patterns of thinking, see Gill, *Personality*, 1.2; on Aristotle's conception of 'deliberation' (a much debated topic), see e.g. J. Lear, *Aristotle: The Desire to Understand* (Cambridge, 1988), pp. 143–51; N. Sherman, *The Fabric of Character: Aristotle's Theory of Virtue* (Oxford, 1989), ch. 3.

18. On Dodds, see n. 2 above. For an alternative reading of Agamemnon's speech, see Ch. III, text to nn. 19–20; for criticism of the idea of 'shame-ethics', as used by Dodds and others, see Ch. III, text to nn. 22–5.

19. See e.g. *Il*. 9. 255–8, 260–1, 496–7, 515–18, 639–42.

20. See e.g. J. Griffin, *Homer on Life and Death* (Oxford, 1980), p. 74. The possible echo of Meleager's response, as presented by Phoenix, in his attempt to persuade Achilles, is noted by C. Whitman, *Homer and the Heroic Tradition* (Cambridge, Mass., 1958), p. 191.

21. See further Gill, *Personality*, 3.3.

22. See *Medea* 1021–80 esp. 1049–55 and 1078–80. The translation of κρείσσων τῶν ἐμῶν βουλευμάτων as 'master of my [revenge] plans' rather than 'stronger than my [ethical] reasonings' is that of a minority of scholars, but seems to me what the sense of the lines (esp. of βουλευμάτων) requires. Difficulties of sense and language lead J. Diggle in the revised Euripides Oxford Classical Text (Oxford, 1984) to excise the whole of 1056–80; but others excise simply all or part of 1056–64. See further C. Gill, 'Two Monologues of Self-Division: Euripides, *Medea* 1021–80 and Seneca, *Medea* 893–977', in M. Whitby, P. Hardie, and M. Whitby, edd., Homo Viator: *Classical Essays for John Bramble* (Bristol, 1987), pp. 25–37; H. Foley, 'Medea's Divided Self', *Classical Antiquity* 8 (1989), 61–85; S. Evans, 'The Self and Ethical Agency in the *Hippolytus* and *Medea* of Euripides', Cambridge Ph.D. thesis, 1994.

23. Another striking instance of this is the use of the language of 'madness' to describe, and to criticize, Ajax's state of mind at a time when he is no longer 'mad' in the ordinary sense of this word: see Sophocles, *Ajax* 610–11, 614–16, 625, 639–40; also R. P. Winnington-Ingram, *Sophocles: An Interpretation* (Cambridge, 1980), pp. 32–8, 42. See also, more generally, S. Goldhill, *Reading Greek Tragedy* (Cambridge, 1986), ch. 7; Gill, 'The Character-Personality Distinction', pp. 17–31.

24. On the relationship between psychological language, ethical debate, and the 'argument' or 'dialectic' of the play see C. Gill, 'The Articulation of the Self in Euripides' *Hippolytus*' in A. Powell, ed., *Euripides, Women, and Sexuality* (London, 1990), pp. 76–107; S. Goldhill, 'Character and Action: Representation and Reading: Greek Tragedy and its Critics', in Pelling, ed., *Characterization*, pp. 100–27.

25. See further Gill, *Personality*, ch. 3, esp. 3.4–5.

26. For the modern theories of mind referred to, see text to nn. 10–15 above. A striking instance is David Charles's reading of Aristotle's account of *akrasia*, *Aristotle's Theory of Action*, chs. 3–4, which uses contemporary action-theory as the basis for a penetrating analysis of Aristotle's treatment. On modern belief-based theories of the emotions, see e.g. A. O. Rorty, ed., *Explaining Emotions* (Berkeley, 1980), chs. 15–21; G. Taylor, *Pride, Shame, and Guilt: Emotions of Self-Assessment* (Oxford, 1985), pp. 1–5; D. L. Cairns, Aidos: *The Psychology and Ethics of Honour and Shame in Ancient Greek Literature* (Oxford, 1993), pp. 5–6, esp. refs. in n. 8. On the problem raised by translating *akrasia* as 'weakness of will', see text to n. 32 below.

27. See *Republic* (*R.*) 439e–441c. See further J. Moline, 'Plato on the Complexity of the Psyche', *AGP* 60 (1978), 1–26; C. Gill, 'Plato and the Education of Character', *AGP* 67 (1985), 1–26; Annas, *Introduction to Plato's* Republic, ch. 5, esp. pp. 124–52; T. Irwin, *Plato's Ethics* (Oxford, 1995), ch. 13, esp. pp. 211–13, 215–22.

28. On Dennett and Plato, see n. 11 above. On Plato and Freud, see A. Kenny, *The Anatomy of the Soul* (Oxford 1973), pp. 10–14; G. X. Santas, *Plato and Freud* (Oxford, 1988); A. W. Price, 'Plato and Freud', in C. Gill, ed., *The Person and the Human Mind: Issues in Ancient and Modern Philosophy* (Oxford, 1990), pp. 247–70; J. Lear, '*Inside and Outside the* Republic', *Phronesis* 38 (1992), 184–215.

29. For the idea that appetites/desires are open to persuasion in this way, see *R.* 554d2–3, e4–5, also 442c10–d1: for the contrasting idea that they are not open to persuasion and need to be suppressed by force (like non-human animals), see 442a6–b3, 589a–b, 591b. See further Gill, *Personality*, 4.2, and refs. in n. 27 above.

30. See *R.* 485d–e, 500b–d, 585b–587a; see further Gill, *Personality*, 4.6. See also Ch. III, text to nn. 69–70.

31. *R.* 500d–501e, 519b–521b: on the issues raised by the latter point, see Ch. III, text to nn. 62–6.

32. Snell, *Scenes from Greek Drama*, pp. 47–56, esp. 56.

33. See Arist. *NE* 7. 3, 1147a24–b19. For analysis, see e.g. D. Wiggins, 'Weakness of Will, Commensurability, and the Objects of Deliberation and Desire', in A. O. Rorty, ed., *Essays on Aristotle's Ethics* (Berkeley, 1980), pp. 241–65, esp. pp. 248–9; Charles, *Aristotle's Philosophy of Action*, ch. 3; J. Gosling, *Weakness of the Will* (London, 1990), ch. 3; A. W. Price, *Mental Conflict* (London, 1995), ch. 3, esp. pp. 132–9.

34. Arist. *NE* 7. 3, 1147a34–b3. See M. F. Burnyeat, 'Aristotle on Learning to be Good', in Rorty, *Essays on Aristotle's* Ethics, pp. 69–92, esp. pp. 82–8; A. O. Rorty, '*Akrasia* and Pleasure: Nicomachean *Ethics* Book 7', in Rorty, *Essays on Aristotle's* Ethics, pp. 267–84, esp. pp. 269–79.

35. On Socrates' theory, see e.g. Gosling, *Weakness of the Will*, chs. 1–2, Price, *Mental Conflict*, ch. 1; for a rather different approach, including a comparison with Freudian theory about neurosis, G. R. F. Ferrari, '*Akrasia* as Neurosis in Plato's *Protagoras*', *Boston Area Colloquium in Ancient Philosophy* 6 (1990), 115–50.

36. See Galen, *De Placitis Hippocratis et Platonis*, ed. De Lacy, with tr. and commentary, 3 vols. (Berlin, 1977–84): IV 1.14–2.44, De Lacy, pp. 238–47, quotation from IV 2.5, De Lacy, pp. 240–1. (De Lacy's edition is a most valuable aid to research on the Stoic theory of the passions, since books IV–V of Galen's work are sources of fundamental importance.) See also A. A. Long and D. N. Sedley, *The Hellenistic Philosophers* (Cambridge, 1987), 2 vols. (=LS), esp. 54 B, J, K. On the theory, see M. Frede, 'The Stoic Doctrine of the Affections of the Soul', in M. Schofield and G. Striker, edd., *The Norms of Nature: Studies in Hellenistic Ethics* (Cambridge, 1986), pp. 93–110; B. Inwood, *Ethics and Human Action in Early Stoicism*, ch. 5; J. Annas, *Hellenistic Philosophy of Mind*, ch. 5; M. Nussbaum, *The Therapy of Desire: Theory and Practice in Hellenistic Ethics* (Princeton, 1994), ch. 10.

37. The later (1st c. A.D.) Stoic Epictetus highlights this aspect of Medea's situation, *Discourses* I. 28. 7–8. A revised Everyman translation of the *Discourses* is now available, by R. Hard, with introduction and notes by C. Gill (London, 1995). On Epictetus' use of Medea as part of his advice on the correct way to use impressions, see A. A. Long, 'Representation and the Self in Stoicism', in Everson, ed., *Psychology*, pp. 102–20, esp. pp. 111–20.

38. Gal. *PHP* IV 2.8–27, De Lacy, pp. 240–5, esp. 27, De Lacy, pp. 244–5, also III 3.13–22, De Lacy, pp. 188–91. For the alternative translation of E. *Med.* 1079, see n. 22 above.

39. See Gal. *PHP* IV 6.19–39, De Lacy, pp. 274–9.

40. On the significance of Chrysippus' reading both for understanding the Stoic theory and the psychology of Medea's monologue, see C. Gill, 'Did Chrysippus Understand Medea?', *Phronesis* 28 (1983), 136–49, and Gill, *Personality*, 3.6. On the extent to which Chrysippus' discussion and related

Stoic texts constitute a theory of *akrasia*, see Gosling, *Weakness of the Will*, ch. 5; Price, *Mental Conflict*, ch. 4.

41. See LS 54 I, K-P.; also I. Kidd, 'Posidonius on Emotions', in A. A. Long, ed., *Problems in Stoicism* (London, 1971), pp. 200–15.

42. This has been argued by J. Fillion-Lahille, *Le De Ira de Seneque et la philosophie stoïcienne des passions* (Paris, 1984), pp. 121–9; J. Cooper, 'Stoic Theories of the Emotions' (unpublished). See further Annas, *Hellenistic Philosophy of Mind*, pp. 118–20, B. Inwood, 'Seneca and Psychological Dualism', in J. Brunschwig and M. C. Nussbaum, edd., *Passions and Perceptions: Studies in Hellenistic Philosophy of Mind* (Cambridge, 1993), pp. 150–83, esp. pp. 153–6; Price, *Mental Conflict*, pp. 175–8. On Galen's own position, see J. Hankinson, 'Actions and Passions: Affection, Emotion and Moral Self-Management in Galen's Philosophical Psychology', in *Passions and Perceptions*, pp. 184–222.

43. On the Epicurean theory of emotions, see Annas, *Hellenistic Philosophy of Mind*, ch. 9. For a survey of ancient philosophical conceptions of therapy, including the Epicurean, see Nussbaum, *Therapy of Desire*. On some related features of Hellenistic thought, see *Passions and Perceptions* (ref. in n. 41 above), esp. Nussbaum, 'Poetry and the Passions: two Stoic Views', pp. 97–149.

44. This emerged in a seminar on ancient and modern approaches to the emotions organized by Richard Sorabji at the British Academy, London, in June 1995, as well as at a seminar organized by him on the therapy of the emotions at Wolfson College, Oxford, in March 1994, Sorabji is preparing a book on the Stoic and Augustinian theories of the passions.

III. ETHICS AND VALUES

In recent work on Greek ethics, several developments parallel, and are linked with, those discussed in Chapter II in connection with psychological models. In this area too, for a variety of reasons, some recent scholarship has laid less stress than before on the idea of development within Greek ethics and on the differences between Greek and modern approaches to ethics. It has emphasized, rather, recurrent patterns in Greek ethical thought of different periods, and also the idea that Greek thought constitutes an intelligible type of ethical thought for modern thinkers. As well as outlining these developments, I suggest ways in which they can be taken further in some ways and qualified in others.[1]

1. *Ethical Development and Greek Culture: Shame and Guilt*

This recent emphasis represents a reaction against a tendency that has been dominant in scholarship on Greek ethics and values for much of the post-war period. This tendency has been to present Greek ethical thinking as a more or less gradual development from 'shame-ethics' to 'guilt-ethics' (to take one favoured model), a tendency sometimes combined with stress on the contrast between Greek and modern forms of ethical thinking. This tendency has its roots in two, rather different, features of twentieth-century scholarly thought. One is the assumption that properly moral thinking centres on certain key ideas and ideals, including those of duty, obligation, the good will, and altruism; and that Greek ethical thinking was primitive or defective in so far as it failed to identify these as its central concerns. This assumption is especially linked with the kind of modern moral thinking based on Kant. The other feature is the extension to ethical values of the anthropological approach which has been, in various forms, widely (though not uniformly) influential in much scholarship on Greek culture in this century, especially in the study of religion and mythology.[2] By contrast with the Kantian approach, anthropology aims to offer an objective or neutral characterization of ethical values in other cultures (or in phases of other cultures). In one, especially influential version, ethical values are treated as part of the *mentalité* or thought-world (system of practices and attitudes) that is characteristic of the culture.[3] Despite the differences between these approaches, they have contributed, separately or in combination, to developmental accounts of Greek ethics which underline its distinctness from modern moral thinking.[4]

In the previous chapter, I noted the way in which Snell's psychological assumptions shaped his view that Greek thought constituted a (gradual and incomplete) development towards the modern – that is, for Snell, the Cartesian or Kantian –conception of the self. The counterpart of this is his view that the Greeks gradually moved towards an understanding of properly moral concepts. Several ideas are crucial for Snell, notably the distinction between 'moral' and 'prudential' consideration (that is, considerations of practical interest or advantage), and also the idea that a properly moral attitude depends on 'the good will', that is, moral intentions. But most important is the assumption that a properly moral response involves the combination of a distinctively individual stance with the recognition that moral principles apply universally. This assumption derives from Kant's famous idea that a moral response involves 'autonomy', that is, binding oneself to universal laws, as opposed to principles which apply to a particular social context or class. For instance, when Homer's Odysseus says that he who would 'be best [aristeuein] in battle must stand his ground strongly, whether he is hit or hits someone else' (Il. 11. 408–10), Snell sees this as a class-based response (what a Homeric 'officer' sees that he must do) not a genuinely moral one.[5] Although he sees a gradual awakening, in the course of Greek ethical history, to the understanding of the universality required in a moral response (especially in Socrates' 'call to virtue'), he thinks that the Greeks never fully grasped the significance of the combination of 'the good will' and universalization.[6]

Similar assumptions underlie Adkins's famous study of Greek values, *Merit and Responsibility* (Oxford, 1960), though his account is also influenced by anthropological and sociological approaches. His presentation of ancient Greece as a 'results-culture' reflects his view, like Snell's, that the Greeks judged people by their success and failure in action rather than by their intentions ('the good will'). Hence, the Greeks failed to distinguish properly between a mistake (a failure in practical calculation) and a moral error, which depends solely on the quality of the will. A related claim is that Greece remained essentially a 'shame-culture', which he understands as one in which ethical status depends on one's standing in the eyes of others rather than on moral intentions. Also, ethical status was predominantly attached not to other-benefiting (or 'cooperative') attitudes, as it is in modern moral thinking, but to 'competitive' values, centred on one's own success. Although Adkins saw the history of Greek culture from Homer to the Stoics and Epicureans as marking the gradual weakening of these tendencies and the beginning of an awareness of the value of intentions and of cooperative values, he saw these as running counter to what remained predominantly a 'shame-culture' and 'results-culture' throughout antiquity.[7]

In some other important studies of ethical development, it is the anthropological, rather than the Kantian, approach that is more in evidence. Dodds's use of the 'shame-guilt' distinction has been immensely influential. Dodds, like Snell and Adkins, associates the idea of 'shame-culture' with an ethical framework which stresses the social status of one's acts rather than individual or internal motives. Unlike them, however, he associates 'guilt' in Greek culture primarily with religious (rather than moral) attitudes. He also locates the change from shame-culture to guilt-culture in the late Archaic and early Classical periods rather than later, seeing it as manifested in the preoccupation with pollution (or blood-guilt) in, for instance, Aeschylean tragedy. This reflects the fact that his understanding of 'guilt' is partly shaped by Freudian psychology and its view of human history. For Dodds, 'guilt' is a matter of the *feeling* of guilt, a not wholly rational response, explained as the social equivalent of the 'super-ego', Freud's version of the idea of 'conscience'.[8] This reflects a different pattern of thinking from Snell and Adkins, for whom the development from shame-ethics or a results-culture is associated with a move towards a more fully rational conception of morality. Like Snell and Adkins, Jean-Pierre Vernant and Suzanne Saïd see this process as a slower and more gradual one, and one that is linked with the development of the political and legal institutions of the *polis*. This view is implied in their picture of fifth-century tragedy as representing a transitional stage between an older, more family-centred view of human agency, and a newer one, stressing the responsibility of individual citizens for their actions. In their accounts, the religious standpoint (presenting human beings as subject to certain kinds of divine forces, such as those linked with the family curse) is associated with the older outlook, rather than the movement from shame to guilt, as it is for Dodds.[9]

It would not be right to say that the developmental approach to Greek values has ceased to be current: I note some more recent examples later (text to nn. 14–17). But there has been sustained and powerful criticism of the kind of developmental accounts summarized so far. Some of this has focused on the historical accuracy of the developmental accounts. Some scholars have, more fundamentally, called into question the contrasts and categories employed in these accounts, and the conception of ethics or morality assumed; in this respect, Williams has again played an important role.

Adkins's claims about Homeric values have been a particular target for criticism. It has been argued that Adkins significantly understates the cooperative dimension of Homeric ethics. It has also been suggested that Adkins's distinction between 'competitive' and 'cooperative' values is fundamentally misleading in this connection, since it is not *any* form of competition that is valued in Homeric society but rather the competitive pursuit of the honour that derives from the (cooperative) defence of family or friendship-group.[10] Adkins's claims about the dominance of competitive values in Homer depend especially on his view that certain Homeric value-terms, especially adjectives, such as *agathos* ('noble' or 'good') are essentially based on status and on success in military and social competition.[11] In a recent and much more thorough study of evaluative vocabulary in Homer, Naoko Yamagata has demonstrated that such language is also used to commend cooperative behaviour and to restrain uncooperative actions and attitudes. She gives special attention to the role of ideas such as *nemesis* ('indignation'), *aidōs* ('shame'), and *eleos* ('pity'), to which Adkins attaches relatively little importance.[12] The point made in the previous chapter about psychological vocabulary also applies on this issue too. This is that we need to study the use of such vocabulary as it functions within Homeric (or other) discourse, if we are to gauge its ethical force accurately.[13]

Another recent development which has a bearing on Adkins's project is the analysis of Greek economic and social relationships in terms of a nexus of types of mutually benefiting reciprocity. Walter Donlan, drawing on the anthropologist Marshall Sahlins, has demarcated a typology of such reciprocities in Homer, as expressed in exchange of objects and services, and in the correlated attitudes and forms of discourse. His principal categories are 'balanced' reciprocity (in which the exchange is, in principle, equal), compensatory (in which the exchange is designed to make up for a previous shortcoming or offence), and 'generalized' reciprocity. The category of 'generalized' reciprocity is of special interest, since it envisages the possibility of return of favours over a period in the course of a potentially extended relationship. In some cases, for instance, when one partner in a reciprocal relationship gives up his life in battle, it is clear that the favour can never be returned, even though the surrender of life is conceived as part of a relationship that is, in principle, reciprocal.[14] Richard Seaford, developing this line of thought in a major study of early Greek culture, has suggested that, in Homeric society reciprocal exchange and religious ritual, working together or in a complementary way, play a role which is analogous to that played by political and legal institutions in later Greek culture.[15] These studies are, like the work of Adkins and the other scholars noted earlier, developmental in approach.[16] But the effect of such studies is to cast further doubt on the 'com-petitive-cooperative' distinction which is central to Adkins's thought. Recip-rocal exchange of gifts and favours in Homeric society is *both* a crucial medium of social cooperation *and* a means by which chieftains gain (com-petitive) status. The complex issues which may arise out of such exchanges, such as that of the ethical status of Achilles' rejection of Agamemnon's gifts in *Il.* 9, derive specifically from this interplay between cooperation and the pursuit of honour.[17]

There have also been substantial criticisms made of Adkins's claims about the lack of an understanding of responsibility in Homer, and about the Homeric inability to distinguish between a mistake and a moral error.[18] It seems clear that Adkins's views on this, like Dodds's views on the externalization of shameful mistakes in Homer, were heavily influenced by a single striking case. This is Agamemnon's speech in *Il.* 19. 77–144, esp. 86–94, in which he says that he was not responsible (*aitios*) for his mis-taken act in taking back Achilles' prize-bride, and that this was the result of the divine power of *atē* ('delusion') which neither gods nor humans can resist.[19] However, Oliver Taplin has argued that Agamemnon's speech should not be taken as a standard example, and as the basis for generaliza-tions about the ethical framework as a whole. Rather, he sees it as an illegitimate use of the idea of divine motivation, by contrast with the more standard idea of (divine and human) 'double-motivation', which does not remove responsibility from the human being performing the action.[20]

Williams, in *Shame and Necessity*, criticizes Adkins's approach in a re-examination of the idea of responsibility for one's actions (chapter 3). He argues that there is no determinate, unitary conception which can be regarded as *the* conception of responsibility. Rather, different ethical frameworks, including the Homeric and the modern Western ones, contain different ways of expressing the idea that people have different degrees and kinds of responsibility for their actions in different circumstances. He suggests that underlying Adkins's distinction between (practical) 'mistake' and 'moral error' is the specifically Kantian distinction between prudential (practical) considerations and moral ones. He also suggests that underlying Adkins's ideas about responsibility is the Kantian idea that human beings have, at a fundamental (or 'transcendental') level, freedom of the will, and that this lies at the root of their moral responsibility for their own actions. If we do not approach the topic with these specific (and very strong) assumptions, the Homeric, and later Greek, framework of thinking about responsibility can seem much more intelligible and coherent.[21] As noted in Chapter II (text to n. 8), Williams argues that Greek tragedy, in particular, is valuable precisely because it embodies the understanding of human ethical experience (recognizing the synthesis of human agency and subjection to outside forces or circumstances) which Williams associates with the ideas of agent regret and moral luck. He argues that these ideas, as embodied in Greek tragedy, remain morally significant for us, as well as for ancient Greeks; and that they are ones which Adkins's Kantian framework fails to acknowledge. More generally, Williams urges scholars to recognize that their accounts (whether developmental or not) of Greek intellectual history rely on philosophical assumptions about the mind and ethics: and that they should recognize the sources of these assumptions and be sure that they wish to retain them.

Williams makes similar points about the 'shame-guilt' distinction, especially when this is used to mark a distinction between a cultural framework in which ethical standards depend on social judgements and one in which they are based on the individual's inner sense of what is right and wrong. He argues, first, that the use of this distinction is, typically, combined with the assumption that the second type of ethical framework is more developed and 'mature'. This assumption reflects, Williams claims, the Kantian belief that a properly moral response requires 'autonomy': that is, the idea that each individual should bind herself to universal laws rather than relying on the ethical framework of her society.[22] D. L. Cairns, in a comprehensive study of shame and honour in Greek culture, argues for a similar view. Cairns goes back beyond Dodds (whose use of the 'shame-guilt' distinction was so influential) to the anthropologists Ruth Benedict and Margaret Mead, who introduced Dodds to the distinction. Cairns argues that their use of the idea of 'guilt culture' gave an undeservedly universal status to a framework of moral thinking (centred on the notions of conscience, guilt, and duty) which is specifically shaped by Protestant forms of Christianity. It is, therefore, a poor basis for cross-cultural analysis, especially when combined with the assumption that guilt-culture is, necessarily, more mature and complex.[23]

Williams and Cairns also argue that the 'shame-guilt' distinction has often been combined with a simplified picture of the way in which shame functions as a moral force. Shame, both in Greek and modern culture, does not depend simply on the force of the social judgements made by other people on one's actions. It also depends on the individual's *internalization* of the ethical judgements made in one's society, so that these become 'one's own' as well as part of the discourse of society. Williams makes special use of the idea of the 'internalized other', the imagined figure who helps the individual to make these judgements at moments of crisis and isolation.

Examples of this 'internalized other' are provided by Polydamas in Hector's deliberative monologue in *Il*. 22. 99–110, and by Telamon, Ajax's father, in a comparable deliberative monologue in Sophocles' *Ajax*, 457–80.[24] Such figures serve to focus a kind of 'shame' which forms part of the individual's own moral thinking (that is, the individual's internalization of his society's thinking). If the complexity and depth expressed in such thinking is recognized, the 'shame-guilt' distinction either breaks down completely, or becomes part of a much more fine-grained account of the relationship between shame-ethics and guilt-ethics than is usually offered.[25]

Another important modern study which bears on the question of developmental accounts of Greek ethics is Alasdair MacIntyre's *After Virtue*. This is a study of modern moral thinking which depends on a certain way of viewing the history of ethical theory from the Greeks onwards. MacInyre argues that ethical theory has no validity unless it is grounded in the attitudes and institutions of a particular community and culture. He is critical of modern theories, such as Kantian or Utilitarian ones, which attempt to provide a universal basis for morality without reference to the ethical framework of specific communities. He is also critical of the prevalent modern idea that the moral life and status of an individual can be defined without taking account of the role that the individual plays in the community, and the nexus of roles and practices that make up the shared life of the community.[26]

In the context of this argument, MacIntyre presents Homeric ethical thinking (by contrast with much modern thought) as valuable precisely because it pictures human life as properly lived in the exercise of those virtues which are appropriately related to the roles and practices of a given community. I noted earlier that Snell presented as relatively primitive the ethical quality of Odysseus' deliberation, because he settled his dilemma in *Il*. 11. 404–10 by reference to what 'cowards do' and what one does who would 'be best' (*aristeuein*) among heroic chieftains. For MacIntyre, this would be, by contrast, a good example of soundly based ethical reasoning, whereas Snell finds missing the universality needed for properly moral decisions.[27] Similarly, MacIntyre commends the kind of ethical theory found in Aristotle, because Aristotle's account of the ethical virtues assumes that such virtues are exercised in, and by the standards of, a specific community. It is true that Aristotle also defines his conception of happiness (*eudaimonia*) by reference to the idea of a generalized 'human nature' (*Nicomachean Ethics* 1.7). But MacIntyre sees this idea as properly based on the forms of communal life and the understanding of the virtues found in specific communities.[28]

Although MacIntyre's argument is formulated in different terms from those of Williams in *Shame and Necessity*, it is complementary to it in certain important ways. If we accept the thrust of MacIntyre's case, we will be unlikely to see a linear movement from a more primitive to a more developed ethical outlook within the history of Greek culture, or between Greek culture and modern culture. Both thinkers highlight ways in which we can see the earliest extant expression of Greek culture, the Homeric poems, as constituting a valid form of ethical thinking. We can connect MacIntyre's emphasis on the communal basis of Homeric ethics with Williams's presentation of the internalization of social judgements as a valid form of ethical motivation.[29] It can be argued that MacInyre gives a simplified account of the extent to which social roles determine individual decisions in Homeric deliberation, and that he has been influenced by those scholars who see Homer as expressing a relatively simple form of shame-ethics.[30] But the non-Kantian philosophical frameworks provided by MacIntyre and Williams can still be seen as providing the basis for a different, and more precise, picture of Homeric and subsequent Greek ethical thinking than is given in the developmental accounts of Snell, Adkins, Dodds, and others of similar views.

2. Greek Ethical Philosophy:
Morality and Happiness, Altruism and Mutual Benefit

In recent scholarship on Greek ethical philosophy, there are partial parallels with the features discussed in the study of Greek poetry and culture. Scholars have also responded, from various standpoints, to the philosophical positions, and the claims about Greek thinking, of Williams and MacIntyre. Earlier this century, it was not uncommon to find scholars presenting Greek philosophy as defective in its ethical thinking, because it failed to recognize the overriding priority of duty (emphasized by Kantian theory) or the overriding priority of other-benefiting, rather than self-benefiting motivation (emphasized by, among other approaches, Utilitarian theory).[31] This is the kind of view that underlies the developmental accounts of Greek thought by Snell and Adkins, which assume that, by these standards, Greek ethical thinking is more or less primitive or defective. This kind of view is much less common in recent scholarship; though they approach the question from differing philosophical standpoints, scholars largely converge in seeing in Greek philosophy a valid type of ethical thinking.

MacIntyre, as just noted, commends Aristotle, by contrast with much modern moral philosophy, for recognizing that general ethical ideas, such as that of human nature, need to be grounded in the ethical practices of a specific community and in the dispositions correlated with these.[32] Williams, in *Ethics and the Limits of Philosophy*, in a broadly similar way, commends Aristotle for recognizing the primacy in ethical life of dispositions developed through interpersonal engagement. He contrasts Aristotle favourably with modern philosophical theories which seek to ground morality on universal ideas such as the rational moral agent (central to Kantian theory) or that of the greatest happiness of the greatest number (a key theme in Utilitarian theory). As he has, famously, put it, he is sceptical of the idea that the 'thick values' which form part of the ethical language of a given community can be grounded in the 'thin values' of general or abstract moral concepts. He also argues that the categories of Greek ethical theory, those of virtue and happiness, provide a more intelligible form of ethical thinking than that of most modern moral theories.[33]

Other scholars, writing from a different intellectual standpoint, argue that Greek ethical theory is closer in its approach to modern theories of the type criticized by MacIntyre and Williams. Terence Irwin, for instance, argues that, although Greek theories take happiness as their goal, they do so in a way that recognizes the overriding claims of moral principles, including the claim on us of benefiting others rather than ourselves. He interprets in this light Plato's argument in the *Republic* (*R.*) that justice (*dikaiosunē*) constitutes happiness (*eudaimonia*). Both here and in Aristotle's ethical theory, he sees evidence of the idea that the deepest kind of 'self-realization' lies in the development of altruism. Whereas MacIntyre and Williams stress the differences between Greek and (most) modern theories, Irwin's approach highlights the similarities, both in the ethical norms assumed, and in the use of general ethical ideas, such as the rational moral agent.[34]

A further and distinct position is taken up by Julia Annas, in *The Morality of Happiness*, a wide-ranging study of ethical thought in Aristotle and Hellenistic philosophy. Annas underlines the differences in general structure between ancient and modern ethical philosophy, while acknowledging that these differences have narrowed with the recent adoption by some modern philosophers of versions of 'virtue ethics'. But she also argue that, within this different structure, Greek thinkers give scope for recognizing the claims of duty and of benefiting others (though not necessarily in the same way and to the same extent as most modern theories).[35] Annas stresses that the starting-point of Greek ethical theory is reflection about one's life as a whole, particularly about its overall goal (*telos*); this is uniformly seen as happiness (*eudaimonia*), though there is much debate among Greek philosophers about what constitutes happiness. Such reflection is seen as being able, if properly carried out, to lead someone to revise her priorities and her understanding of happiness. This type of reflection often involves an appeal to what it is 'natural' for human beings to take as their goal, an appeal that might also involve the revision of the conventional understanding of what is 'natural'. So far, it may not seem that Annas's picture contains much that modern thinkers would regard as specifically moral. However, Annas also stresses that most Greek philosophers give an important, and sometimes central, role to virtue in their accounts of happiness. They also conceive virtue, and happiness, as allowing scope for other-concern (including other-concern of a deep or extensive kind). In this way, Greek philosophical accounts of the pursuit of one's own happiness provide a framework which validates much of what we would regard as 'morality'.

I think that Annas's book, as well as illuminating a wide range of Greek theories, also provides what is, in many ways, a highly convincing general characterization of Greek ethical thinking. But there are certain points which I would present in a rather different way. For instance, I would lay greater stress on the idea that Greek ethical reflection is, characteristically, conceived as shared debate or dialectic (rather than individual reflection), and debate about a (shared) human happiness or nature (rather than about *my* life as a whole). I would also stress rather more the idea that such debate is conceived as partly extending, and partly counteracting, the guidance about goals of action and life contained in pre-reflective discourse between people and within communities. These two points contribute to what I see as a dominant image in Greek thought: that of human beings as situated in three interconnected types of dialogue or discourse: reflective debate, interactive exchange, and the 'dialogue' between the parts of the personality.[36] I would also present rather differently the way that other-concern is conceived in Greek thought. I think that it is seen as arising in a framework in which the interpersonal norm is that of mutual benefit (through shared life or reciprocity) rather than altruism; and that this fact marks a significant difference between Greek and modern ethical thought.[37]

A further general point that I would make is this. I think that it is possible to demarcate in Greek philosophy two broad patterns of thinking about ethical development and the shaping of character that forms part of this development. In the first pattern, full ethical development consists of an integrated, two-stage process: first, the development of sound dispositions and practical reasoning through involvement in proper interpersonal and communal relationships; second, reflective debate, leading ultimately to objective ethical knowledge, of a kind which can reshape one's character and life. Versions of this pattern can be found in Plato's *Republic*, Aristotle's ethical theory, and in certain strands of Stoic theory. In the alternative pattern, it is emphasized that (successful) reflective debate is a prerequisite for proper forms of interpersonal and communal relationships as well as for the proper shaping of character and way of life. This pattern is clearest in Epicurean theory; but versions of it can be found in some Platonic dialogues, especially the *Phaedo*, and in other strands of Stoic thought.[38]

I now outline certain issues which illustrate these recent scholarly approaches to Greek ethical philosophy, including, where appropriate, the patterns of thinking that I have just emphasized The first set of issues are those relating to Platonic theories of love, and Aristotelian and Epicurean theories of friendship. The second set of issues relates to the question whether practical or theoretical wisdom constitutes the highest form of human happiness; I consider ways in which this issue arises in Plato's *Republic* and in Aristotle.

3. *Greek Theories of Love and Friendship*

In a famous article, Gregory Vlastos expressed a view of Platonic love which is characteristic of some earlier scholarship: namely, that Plato's ideal fails to grasp the crucial feature of love, namely love of an individual for his own sake. His criticism is directed especially at the climax of the main speech in the *Symposium*, namely the 'mysteries' of Diotima, as reported by Socrates (210–12). This depicts an 'ascent' of desire, which leads, on the face of it, beyond interpersonal love to love of an object of knowledge, the Form of the Beautiful (*kalon*).[39] However, several subsequent scholars, notably A. W. Price, have argued that the account of the mysteries of Diotima allows more than one possible interpretation. In particular it is possible that the ascent of desire may be carried out in company with (possibly) one loved person, with whom one carries out the 'procreation' of virtue that brings about one's own immortalization.[40] In other words, the mysteries can be seen as conveying an ideal in which interpersonal relationships are deepened by a growing understanding of ethical truth, rather than one in which love of knowledge replaces love of other people.[41]

This type of interpretation is, clearly, appropriate for the myth about love and the *psuchē* in the *Phaedrus*, in which continuing love-partnerships are explicitly discussed;[42] it is also a possible way of reading the mysteries of Diotima. A further possibility is that Diotima's ascent of desire is, as traditionally supposed, one which leads beyond love directed at particular people to love directed at knowledge of truth; but that the outcome of the ascent is *not* that one turns away from other people and retains the benefit of this knowledge for oneself. Rather, the outcome is to make one want to communicate to other people (other people generally, rather than a parti-cular loved person) that this form of knowledge constitutes the highest form of human love and happiness. In this way, Socrates, who has been led to this knowledge by Diotima, communicates to the others present at the symposium an account of the ascent of desire in which the lover is led through the stages of the ascent by a more knowledgeable guide.[43] On this reading, the mysteries of Diotima exemplify a pattern which is, I think, recurrent in Greek ethical philosophy. In this pattern, although the out-come of ethical reflection is not to validate what is conventionally taken to be other-benefiting action, *communicating* the kind of life validated by reflection (here, the philosophical life) is seen as the most profound way to benefit others.[44]

Aristotle's theory of friendship raises some broadly comparable issue. On the one hand, Aristotle seems to presume as conventional the idea that friendship, at its best, is altruistic: one wishes the friend well 'for his sake not one's own' (*NE* 8. 1–2). In presenting his own ideal form of friendship (that between two virtuous people), Aristotle offers his own formulation of this idea: one wishes the friend well for what he is 'in himself' (*NE* 8. 3–5). On the other hand, Aristotle presents the friendship between two good people as valuable because it constitutes a context for (virtuous) self-love and a means of perpetuating one's own (virtuous) happiness. It does so because the virtuous person, by being a good friend, realizes his true self ('what each of us is', as a virtuous person). He also extends his own happiness by treating the virtuous friend as an 'other self' (*allos autos*, and by taking as much pleasure in the other's virtue as in his own (*NE* 9. 4, 8, 9).[45] This combination of features has sometimes been found problematic because Aristotle seems both to presuppose (and to build on) an altruistic ideal of friendship, which he subsequently analyses in egoistic terms.[46] A response made by some recent discussions is to argue that Aristotle's analysis of ideal friendship presupposes, and depends on, the ideal of altruism, rather than undermining this. It is only if the friendship involved *is* altruistic (if one regard the other as a 'second self', in the full sense, and if one identifies as one's true self the virtuous and other-benefiting self) that virtuous friendship promotes one's happiness in the way that Aristotle claims.[47] In *The Morality of Happiness*, Annas further claims that Aristotle's account of the relationship between self-love and other-benefiting friendship constitutes a distinct theory about the way in which other-benefiting motivation develops. Although Aristotle's account implies that self-love is, in some sense, a more primary kind of motivation, it also implies that, in a full process of ethical development, it can provide the basis for the development of fully other-benefiting motivation.[48]

These recent discussions combine philosophically powerful argumentation with close reading of the relevant texts. However, I would like to register some reservations about this line of thought. I think that interpretation of Aristotle's argument should be placed, as far as possible, against the background of the norm of interpersonal ethics current in the relevant culture. In Greece, this is, arguably, not so much altruism as the kind of relationship that brings mutual benefit to both partners, either through the 'shared life' of the family and close friendship or through reciprocation of favours and benefits. Some of Aristotle's comments about conventional ideals of friendship seem to presuppose these ideas;[49] and, in formulating his own version of these ideals, he stresses the thought that the friendship of two good people (his ideal) confers maximal benefit on both partners.[50] In reflecting on the implications of this ideal for the relationship between virtue and happiness (*NE* 9. 4, 8, 9, *EE* 7. 6, 12), the main thrust of his remarks seems to be that, if friendship is fully combined with virtue, even the most extreme demands of friendship are fully compatible with the realization of one's own happiness. Thus, friendship, even when requiring, in the most extreme case, that one should give up one's life for a friend, is compatible with the best possible (most virtuous) character and way of life, and thus confers maximal benefit on the person acting in this way. Aristotle's thinking, as so interpreted, forms an intelligible continuation of the heroic ideal of the cooperative pursuit of honour discussed earlier in this chapter; and both ideals can be seen as implying the norm of mutual benefit, through shared life or reciprocity, rather than altruism.[51]

A comparable set of issues has been discussed in connection with an apparent conflict that arises in Epicurean thinking about friendship. On the one hand, Epicureans hold that one should 'take risks' for the sake of friendship, and that the ideal ('wise') person will 'never give up' a friend, and 'will on occasion die for a friend'.[52] On the other hand, Epicurus stresses that the virtues (presumably, including the virtues associated with friendship) should be regarded as instrumental means to realize the overall goal in life (that of pleasure, as Epicurus conceives this). He also stresses that you should 'refer each of your actions on every occasion to nature's end' (that is, to the overall goal of pleasure).[53] There is reason to think that the Epicureans themselves were aware of this as an inconsistency or conflict and offered various ways of resolving it. Epicurus' position, as far as we can determine this, seems to be that, considered over a lifetime, friendship provides a means for fulfilling the Epicurean goals, both because it offers a guarantee of help and security and because it is a positive source of 'joy'.[54] However, friendship only serves as an effective means of achieving this goal, if the friendship involved is, in a sense to be considered, a 'real' friendship. In such a friendship, 'we rejoice in our friend's joy as much as in our own and we are equally pained by their distress', and so are willing to undergo the pain and troubles that may be part of any close and demanding friendship.[55]

However, there arises here, as in Aristotle's theory about friendship, the question of what counts as a 'real' friendship. If the question is framed in terms of a contrast between egoism and altruism, and the demand is that friendship be wholly altruistic, then the conflict with Epicurus' (egoistic) advocacy of the overall goal of pleasure may be, in the end, insoluble.[56] However, for Epicurus, as for Aristotle, there are indications that the norm presupposed is that of mutual benefit conferred by shared life or reciprocity rather than altruism. Thus, Epicurus criticizes *both* someone 'who is always looking for help' out of friendship *and* 'one who never associates help with friendship' and who, therefore, 'cuts off confident expectation in regard to the future' (LS 22 F(4)). Also, the best kind of friendship, for Epicurus, is one in which the lives of both partners are shaped by Epicurean objectives. So, while in an Aristotelian ideal friendship, virtuous people work for each other's good, in an ideal Epicurean friendship, the friend 'will take the same trouble for his friend's *pleasure* as he would for his own' (LS 22 O(3)). Similarly, when friendship is terminated by death, we should express our fellow-feeling for friends, not by 'grieving' for them (since, for an Epicurean, 'death is nothing to us'), but by 'thinking' about them in a way that prolongs the pleasure that makes friendship 'an immortal good'.[57] This kind of friendship is a 'real' one both in the sense that friends will take trouble on each other's behalf and that 'each of [their] actions [can be referred] on every occasion to nature's end', that is, to pleasure, as Epicurus understands this.[58] In other words, a friendship of this type is characterized not simply by mutual benefit but by (what Epicureans see as) the deepest available understanding of what mutual benefit involves.

4. *Practical versus Contemplative Wisdom*

I turn now to two famous passages, in Plato and in Aristotle, which raise similar issues about the ethical thinking involved; they do so in connection with the rival claims of practical and theoretical wisdom to count as the highest form of human happiness. In the *Republic*, after describing the two-stage educational programme of the philosopher-rulers, Plato indicates that the rulers may be reluctant to leave the philosophical contemplation of truth to 're-enter the cave' of practical, political action in which they will use the knowledge gained through their education. He suggests, several times, that the philosopher-rulers will need to be 'compelled' to do so.[59] The use of the language of compulsion is puzzling because it is not the reaction we might expect from philosopher-rulers to the prospect of fulfilling their role of 'taking care of the city as a whole'.[60] Also, the language of compulsion is at odds with the point also made that, when it is explained to the philosopher-rulers why they should re-enter the cave, they will be 'not unwilling', and perhaps 'keen', to do so.[61]

This passage is also puzzling because it seems to raise questions about Plato's basic project in the *Republic*, that of showing that justice (as described in the *Republic*) constitutes happiness. The philosopher-rulers, the product of the two-stage educational programme, represent the highest grade of ethical character in the *Republic*; if they are less than fully motivated towards their proper role, this calls into question the coherence of the whole theory.[62] This point has received special attention in recent years, because it seems to run counter to the present general view that Greek philosophy embodies an approach which is 'ethical' or 'moral' in a sense that modern thinkers too can recognize. Irwin, for instance, argues that Plato is mistaken in suggesting that the philosopher-rulers might be reluctant to re-enter the cave. He outlines an interpretation of Plato's theory (based partly on the analogy with Diotima's theory of love in the *Symposium*, as Irwin interprets this), which shows that the philosopher-rulers should be positively motivated to use their knowledge of ethical truths in other-benefiting action.[63]

On any interpretation, it is clear that Plato's presentation goes some way towards resolving this problem by saying that, if it is explained to the philosopher-rulers why they should re-enter the cave, 'they surely won't refuse ... or be unwilling to take their turn in joining the work in the city?'. They will react in this way, because 'we shall be making a just demand of just people' (520d6–e1). To this extent, despite the talk of 'compulsion' elsewhere, it is made plain that the philosopher-rulers will be 'just' in the sense of 'not unwilling' to play the role for which they have been pre-pared.[64] The philosopher-rulers' response is not, I think, best understood as that of altruism, if this means that one's highest priority is to benefit others for its own sake. Plato's language suggests, rather, a type of reciprocal exchange: unlike philosophers in other states, the philosopher-rulers in the ideal state should 'be keen to pay back the cost of their upbringing [$\dot{\epsilon}\kappa\tau\dot{\iota}\nu\epsilon\iota\nu$ . . . $\tau\grave{\alpha}$ $\tau\rho o\phi\epsilon\hat{\iota}\alpha$]', which has made them uniquely capable of both philo-sophical knowledge and government (520b). The ethical model of reci-procity allows the idea, as the model of altruism does not, that the philosopher-rulers, in making this response to the claims of others, are also giving up something that is more inherently desirable. This is the philo-sophical contemplation which, other things being equal, they would prefer to continue.[65] But, like Homeric heroes who are ready to enter battle and to risk their lives as an act of 'generalized' reciprocity in return for proper honour from their comrades and people, the philosopher-rulers are willing to do so in return for their special education and status.[66]

However, to make full sense of the ambivalence in Plato's presentation of the attitude of the philosopher-rulers to re-entering the cave, we need to take into account the two-stage programme of ethical education, and the (complex) outcome of this for the character of the philosopher-rulers. The first stage of this programme can be understood as the 'internalization' (to re-use this notion here) of communal beliefs and standards by the young guardians, and the associated shaping of aspirations and desires.[67] The second stage provides the analytic understanding of those beliefs and standards, and the basis for applying them in shaping the life of the com-munity.[68] However, there is a further dimension in the second stage. As well as enabling the philosopher-rulers to understand communal standards and virtue, it also confers virtues of a different and deeper kind which depend directly on the possession of philosophical knowledge. In the case of temperance or moderation (sōphrosunē), for instance, the awareness of the superior pleasures of philosophical understanding reshapes the philo-sopher's pattern of desires in a way that goes beyond the conventional form of moderation of sensual desires.[69] Implied in this point (as in the argu-ments about the rival merits of different pleasures)[70] is the idea that the philosophical understanding of truth constitutes the highest possible human activity, and that the philosopher's character and pattern of motivation reflect this fact. It follows from this that philosopher-rulers will, indeed, be giving up an activity that is inherently more desirable in undertaking the other aspect of their role, that of exercising their knowledge in political action, though they are also strongly motivated to undertake this political role. Plato's ambivalent presentation of the attitude of the philosopher-rulers thus corresponds precisely to the motivation that the theory requires, one that gives highest value to philosophical knowledge of truth, without denying the value of practical action based on such knowledge.[71]

A passage in Aristotle which raises similar issues is *Nicomachean Ethics* 10. 7–8, which argues that theoretical or contemplative wisdom constitutes the highest (more 'divine') form of happiness, by contrast with the 'human' happiness of practical wisdom combined with ethical virtue, which is also valued but less highly. Scholars differ sharply about this passage.[72] Some hold that Aristotle's move here, that of determining a 'dominant' form of happiness, is inconsistent with the general approach of *NE* (as expressed in 1. 7, for instance), which implies an 'inclusive' conception of happiness, including practical and contemplative aspects.[73] Others hold that Aristotle's move is consistent with the overall shape and structure of his argument in *NE*, with the preference of contemplative over practical wisdom in *NE* 6, and with Aristotle's metaphysical conception of god and the divine.[74] I am more persuaded by the latter approach, although I think that Aristotle also acknowledges the tension created by the rival claims of practical wisdom, and implies a way of resolving this tension (in so far as it is resolvable).

One reason why scholars have expressed reservations about Aristotle's explicit preference for contemplative wisdom in *NE* 10. 7–8 is, I think, because it contradicts our modern view of what a moral theory should establish. The second-class 'human' life is the one that involves our performing 'just, brave, and other virtuous actions towards each other' (*NE* 10. 8, 1178a10–11); and, by contrast, the preference for the contemplative life may seem to be an egoistic one. Richard Kraut, however, while assuming that it is appropriate to analyse Aristotle's theory in terms of egoism and altruism,[75] argues that Aristotle's theory need not be taken as egoistic. He points out that Aristotle assumes that, even if someone (properly) takes contemplative wisdom as the highest possible activity and goal of one's life, 'in so far as he is a human being and shares his life with a number of people, he chooses to act in accordance with [ethical] virtue'.[76] Indeed, in presenting the exercise of practical wisdom in conjunction with ethical virtue as the essentially 'human' function, 10. 7–8 gives a high, if not the highest, value to this type of virtue. Also, contemplation is itself conceived by Aristotle as a sociable, cooperative activity.[77]

I think that this line of thought can be developed (and in a way that fits in better with Greek patterns of ethical thinking) by reference to the idea put forward earlier in connection with Plato's *Symposium*. This is that to communicate the truth about the nature of the highest human happiness is the most profound way to benefit other people, even if the truth communicated is not the validation of other-benefiting virtue (as ordinarily understood). Aristotle can, indeed, be seen as motivated to benefit his audience in this way, just as Socrates is motivated to do as a result of his initiation in the 'mysteries' of Diotima. In both cases, and also (though less explicitly) in the philosopher-rulers' re-entry to the cave, the truth conveyed is that of the ultimate preferability of contemplative wisdom as a mode of human happiness.[78] This line of thought can be supported by Sarah Broadie's suggestion that *NE* 10. 7–8 makes most sense when read as an argument directed at those who already see the value of virtuous practical reasoning and who will readily accept the idea that such a life is the essentially 'human' one.[79] What Aristotle seeks to show such an audience is that, as *NE* claims, contemplative wisdom is still higher and more 'divine', but it does so in a way that does not radically devalue virtuous practical wisdom. In the context of such a discussion, the claim that contemplative reason constitutes our 'true self' ('what each of us is') rather than the practical reason that is presented in this way in 9. 4 and 9. 8 might be taken as a deliberate *re*definition of the idea of the 'true self'.[80] Given that, as seems clear from *NE* 10. 7–8, Aristotle regards contemplative wisdom as our 'divine' (highest and most essential) function, to persuade other virtuous people of this truth is to benefit them in the same way as this knowledge benefits oneself.[81] This reading of 10. 7–8 both gives weight to its explicit claims, taken in the context of *NE* as a whole, and allows the discussion to have an other-benefiting function in a way that is compatible with the ethical framework found elsewhere in Greek thought.

In the latter part of this chapter (sections 2–4), I have tried to illustrate ways in which recent scholarship on Greek ethical theory has tended to interpret this as being compatible with modern thinking about morality and the role of moral theory. This tendency is partly parallel to that discussed in the first section of this chapter, in which certain kinds of developmental approaches to Greek values have been criticized, and partly replaced, by approaches which stress the continuing ethical intelligibility of Greek poetry, especially Homer and Greek tragedy, to modern thinkers.[82] For the most part, I support this recent approach to Greek ethical philosophy, and have indicated ways in which it can be taken further. However, I have expressed reservations about the tendency to ascribe to Greek ethical theory a similar valuation of altruism to that found in modern thought. Although Greek thought seems clearly to give an important place to other-benefiting acts and attitudes, this type of motivation is located in a framework in which shared, mutual, or reciprocated benefit, rather than altruism, are standardly taken as norms of interpersonal ethics.[83] I return to ethical themes later in this book, in connection with political ideas in Ch. IV and the idea of nature as a norm in Ch. V.

NOTES

1. My main qualification is the suggestion that Greek ethical thinking does not give the same central value to altruism as modern ethical thinking, though it provides an alternative framework in which other-benefiting motivation can be accommodated. See below, text to nn. 37, 49–58, 65–6.

2. On the latter point, see J. N. Bremmer, *Greek Religion* (Oxford, 1994), p. 56.

3. See further G. E. R. Lloyd, *Demystifying Mentalities* (Cambridge, 1990). The most famous exponents of the *mentalité* approach, which is associated with structural anthropology, are the members of the 'Paris school', e.g. J.-P. Vernant, P. Vidal-Naquet, M. Detienne.

4. The intellectual background of modern anthropological thinking about the mapping of concepts (including the influence of Kantian and post-Kantian thinking) is illuminated by S. Collins in an essay on the approach of the anthropologist, M. Mauss, to cross-cultural study of the concept of self: see M. Carrithers, S. Collins, S. Lukes, edd., *The Category of the Person: Anthropology, Philosophy, History* (Cambridge, 1985), pp. 46–82.

5. See *The Discovery of the Mind*, p. 159, taken in the context of pp. 154–61: Snell compares Odysseus' response to that of an 'officer' who gauges 'his action by the rigid conception of honour peculiar to his caste'.

6. Snell, *The Discovery of the Mind*, ch. 8, esp. pp. 154–60, 163–4, 165–7, 167–70, 182–3, 186–8. For a succinct statement of Kant's ideas about the good will and autonomy (i.e. self-legislation), see the translation of *The Groundwork of the Metaphysic of Morals* in H. J. Paton, *The Moral Law* (London, 1986), pp. 59–70.

7. See *Merit and Responsibility*, esp. pp. 1–9, including Adkins's notorious claim, p. 2, that, in our moral thinking, 'we are all Kantians now'. On 'mistake and moral error', see his ch. 3, including the distinction between competitive and cooperative values on pp. 34–8. A similar view is advanced in Adkins, *From the Many to the One* (London, 1970), which also discusses the (partial) reaction against shame ethics in Stoicism and Epicureanism, pp. 237–8, 259–60.

8. See *The Greeks and the Irrational* (Berkeley, 1951), esp. ch. 2, pp. 36–7, 47–9. My account spells out rather more explicitly than Dodds what I take to be the Freudian basis of this approach (though Dodds does allude to Freud in this connection, e.g. p. 49).

9. See Ch. II, n. 4.

10. See e.g. A. A. Long, 'Morals and Values in Homer', *JHS* 90 (1970), 121–39; H. Lloyd-Jones, *The Justice of Zeus* (Berkeley, 1971), p. 15; C. J. Rowe, 'The Nature of Homeric Morality', in A. C. Rubino and C. W. Shelmerdine, edd., *Approaches to Homer* (Austin, 1983), pp. 248–75. To say this is not to deny that difficult ethical issues can arise in connection with the interplay between cooperation and the pursuit of honour, a point stressed, with reference to both Homer's Achilles and Hector, by J. Redfield, *Nature and Culture in the* Iliad: *The Tragedy of Hector* (Chicago, 1975, 2nd edn., Durham, N.C., 1994.); see also Ch. IV, text to nn. 12–23.

11. See *Merit and Responsibility*, pp 30–46. E.g. Adkins takes the words spoken by Nestor to Agamemnon about the latter's proposal to take away Achilles' prize-bride in *Il.* 1. 131–2, 'Do not, good [or 'noble', *agathos*] though you are, take the girl from him', as supporting his view that being noble (*agathos*) is independent of, or can legitimate, uncooperative behaviour (pp. 37–8).

12. N. Yamagata, *Homeric Morality* (Leiden, 1994), part 2, esp. chs. 9–11. Yamagata also highlights ways in which terms such as *agathos*, *aristos* ('best'), and *kakos* ('poor', 'bad') do not only signify social standing in Homer, but also evaluate the range of qualities (both cooperative and competitive) associated with social standing: see e.g. pp. 191–2, 205–6, 211–12.

13. See Ch. II, text to nn. 18–25. On this point, see also K. J. Dover, *Greek Popular Morality in the Time of Plato and Aristotle* (Oxford, 1974), pp. 14–18, and 'The Portrayal of Moral Evaluation in

Greek Poetry', *JHS* 103 (1983), 35–48; also M. Nussbaum, *The Fragility of Goodness* (Cambridge, 1986), pp. 424–5 n. 20; S. Goldhill, *Reading Greek Tragedy* (Cambridge, 1986), pp. 122–7.

14. W. Donlan, 'Reciprocities in Homer', *Classical World* 75 (1981–2), 137–75; 'The Unequal Exchange between Glaucus and Diomedes in the Light of the Homeric Gift-Economy', *Phoenix* 43 1989), 1–15; 'Duelling with Gifts in the *Iliad*: As the Audience Saw It', *Colby Quarterly* 29 (1993), 155–72. For a rather different model, based on the contrast between 'positive' and 'negative' reciprocity, see A. W. Gouldner, 'The Norm of Reciprocity: A Preliminary Statement', *American Sociological Review* 25 (1960), 161–78, reprinted in *For Sociology: Renewal and Critique in Sociology Today* (New York, 1973), pp. 226–59.

15. R. Seaford, *Reciprocity and Ritual: Homer and Tragedy in the Developing City-State* (Oxford, 1994); see esp. his pp. 65–73 and ch. 5. on *Il.*

16. See further C. Gill, N. Postlethwaite, and R. Seaford, edd., *Reciprocity in Ancient Greece* (Oxford, forthcoming), which explores the question how far the practices and thought-patterns associated with reciprocity in Homer persist in subsequent Greek culture. See further on this question Ch. IV, text to n. 6.

17. On this see Donlan, 'Duelling with Gifts'; see further Ch. IV, text to nn. 12–23.

18. See text to n. 7 above.

19. See Adkins, *Merit and Responsibility*, pp. 50–2; Dodds, *The Greeks and the Irrational*, ch. 1, esp. pp. 2–8.

20. See O. Taplin, 'Agamemnon's Role in the *Iliad*', in Pelling, ed., *Characterization*, pp. 60–82, esp. pp. 75–7; *Homeric Soundings: The Shaping of the* Iliad (Oxford, 1992), pp. 207–10. As Taplin notes, Achilles' words in 19. 270–5 restore the more normal Homeric pattern of combined divine and human motivation. On divine intervention and 'double-motivation', the best study remains A. Lesky, *Göttliche und menschliche Motivation im homerischen Epos* (Heidelberg, 1961). Similar non-standard uses of the idea of divine power over human action are found in Euripides, *Trojan Women* 945–50, and Gorgias, *Encomium of Helen* 15, 19–20; see S. Saïd, *La Faute tragique* (Paris, 1978), pp. 193–9, 252–7.

21. B. Williams, *Shame and Necessity* (Berkeley, 1993), ch. 3, esp. pp. 52–8, 66–8; see also pp. 41–4, 98–102, 158–63, on the influence of Kantian ideas about the will, freedom, and autonomy, taken with refs. to Adkins in Williams's index. (William sees this latter type of idea as being also Platonic; for a different view on this point, see Gill, *Personality in Greek Epic, Tragedy, and Philosophy* (Oxford, 1996), 6.6.)

22. Williams, *Shame and Necessity*, ch. 4, esp. pp. 75–8, 91–5, 97–8.

23. D. L. Cairns, Aidos: *The Psychology and Ethics of Honour and Shame in Ancient Greek Literature* (Oxford, 1993), pp. 27–47.

24. Williams, *Shame and Necessity*, ch. 4, esp. pp. 81–98. The idea of the 'internalized other' is one that he sees as capable of playing a role in modern versions of 'shame-ethics'; it is drawn from G. Taylor, *Pride, Shame and Guilt: Emotions of Self-Assessment* (Oxford, 1985), pp. 53–68. On the deliberative ethical thinking of Hector and Ajax, see further Gill, *Personality*, 1.4 and 3.4.

25. Cairns, Aidos, pp. 15–26, 141–6, argues that the distinction breaks down completely; Williams, *Shame and Necessity*, pp. 88–95, argues that there are two forms of (equally complex) ethical thinking involved. For an earlier, and less analytic, critique of the 'shame-guilt' distinction, see Lloyd-Jones, *Justice of Zeus*, ch. 1, esp. pp. 24–7.

26. A. MacIntyre, *After Virtue: A Study in Moral Theory* (London, 1985, 2nd edn.), esp. chs. 1–8, 14–18. On the relevance of the latter idea to the study of Greek thinking, see also Ch. IV, section 1.

27. On Snell, see text to nn. 5–6 above. See MacIntyre, *After Virtue*, ch. 10, on Homeric ethics. MacIntyre does not discuss this particular passage there; he notes it in *Whose Justice? Which Rationality?* (London, 1988), pp. 15–16, in connection with Homeric ethical thinking.

28. See MacIntyre, *After Virtue*, ch. 12; for the contrast between Aristotle and modern theories, beginning with Kant, which MacIntyre sees as trying to ground ethical standards by reference to universal norms alone (without the mediation of communal values), see his chs. 4–6. See further Ch. V, text to nn. 6–11.

29. See further Gill, *Personality*, 1.3–4.

30. MacIntyre, *After Virtue*, p. 122, refers to M. I. Finley, *The World of Odysseus* (London, 1954), ch. 5, which overstates the role-governed nature of Homeric society and the extent to which this minimizes the scope for rational deliberation. For a critique of Finley on this point, see M. Schofield, '*Euboulia* in Homer', *CQ* NS 36 (1986), 6–31.

31. See e.g. H. A. Prichard, *Moral Obligation and Duty and Interest* (Oxford, 1968), esp. chs. 1 and 3,

published versions of papers first given in 1912 and 1935; W. D. Ross, *Aristotle* (Oxford, 1923), esp. p. 208; G. J. Warnock, *The Object of Morality* (London, 1971), pp. 89–92.

32. See text to n. 28 above.

33. B. Williams, *Ethics and the Limits of Philosophy* (London, 1985), esp. chs. 3–5, 10; on 'thick values', see pp. 143–5. For a thoughtful critique of Williams on this point, see S. Scheffler, 'Morality through Thick and Thin', *Philosophical Review* 96 (1987), 411–34. Both Williams and MacIntyre acknowledge that Aristotle, in *NE* 1.7, gives the general idea of human nature a role in ethical theory; see further Ch. V, section 1.

34. See esp. T. Irwin, *Plato's Moral Theory* (Oxford, 1977), ch. 7, which explores the relationship between 'eudaimonistic' (happiness-centred theories) and 'deontological' (duty-centred) ones; also *Plato's Ethics* (Oxford, 1995), esp. chs. 17–18; *Aristotle's First Principles* (Oxford, 1988), chs. 16–18. A broadly similar position is adopted by T. Engberg-Pedersen, *Aristotle's Theory of Moral Insight* (Oxford, 1983); *The Stoic Theory of* Oikeiosis (Aarhus, 1990). See further Gill, *Personality*, 4.3, 5.2.

35. See J. Annas, *The Morality of Happiness* (Oxford, 1993), esp. Introduction and ch. 22. On modern forms of virtue-ethics, see her pp. 7–10.

36. See Gill, *Personality*, subtitle *The Self in Dialogue*, esp. Introd, and ch. 6, where I present this image as expressing an 'objective-participant' conception of human personality; for examples of the interplay between two or more of these types of dialogue, see Ch. II, text to nn. 19–25, 27–31; see also Ch. VI, text to nn. 6–12.

37. See Gill, *Personality*, 5.3; also 'Altruism or Reciprocity in Greek Ethical Philosophy?', in Gill, Postlethwaite, Seaford, edd., *Reciprocity in Ancient Greece* (forthcoming). Annas also expresses unease about the use of the notion of 'altruism' in connection with Greek ethical theory, pp. 225–6, an unease which I would reinforce. I accept that Greek ethical thought does provide a framework for explaining, and validating (what we should see as) 'other-concern' (the main theme of Annas, *Morality of Happiness*, part 3), though I think that Greek assumptions about interpersonal ethics mean that this process is conceived rather differently by them. An alternative move is to de-emphasize the difference between the ideals of altruism and mutual benefit, and thus to present Greek thought as closer to modern ethics than I am suggesting: see e.g. C. Kahn, 'Aristotle and Altruism', *Mind* 90 (1981), 20–40, esp. pp. 21–7; R. Kraut, *Aristotle on the Human Good* (Princeton, 1989), pp. 78–86; on reciprocity and altruism as ideals which can be combined, see Gouldner, *For Sociology* (ref. in n. 14 above), p. 246.

38. See Gill, *Personality*, 4.5, 5.7, and 6.6–7. See further text to nn. 52–8, 67–71, 78–81 below; see also Ch. V, sections 3–4; and, for an analogous division in Greek patterns of thinking about the best form of community, see Ch. IV, text to nn. 10–11.

39. G. Vlastos, 'The Individual as an Object of Love in Plato', first given as a paper in 1969, in Vlastos, *Platonic Studies* (Princeton, 1981, 2nd edn.), pp. 3–42, esp. pp. 30–4. For this type of criticism of Greek ethical thinking, see text to n. 31 above. Vlastos's view is partly adopted and partly qualified (by reference to Alcibiades' speech) in M. C. Nussbaum, *The Fragility of Goodness* (Cambridge, 1986), ch. 6. For a review of the debate about the conception of love expressed in the *Symposium*, see C. Gill, 'Platonic Love and Individuality', in A. Loizou and H. Lesser, edd., Polis *and Politics: Essays in Greek Moral and Political Philosophy* (Aldershot, 1990), pp. 69–88.

40. For self-immortalization and procreation of virtue, see esp. *Symposium (Smp.)* 206a–b, 207d–209e, 212a. It is clear that there may be at least one change of partner in the course of the ascent, from one who is beautiful in body to one who is beautiful in mind (210b6–c6); but the latter partner *may* be retained throughout the rest of the ascent, and may be the recipient of educative discourse at 210d5 and 212a5–7.

41. See A. W. Price, *Love and Friendship in Plato and Aristotle* (Oxford, 1989), ch. 2, esp. pp. 38–54; also 'Martha Nussbaum's *Symposium*', *Ancient Philosophy* 11 (1991), 285–99, esp. pp. 289–90. See also L. Kosman, 'Platonic Love', in W. H. Werkmeister, ed., *Facets of Plato's Philosophy* (Assen, 1976), pp. 53–69; T. Irwin, *Plato's Moral Theory*, pp. 234–7, *Plato's Ethics*, ch. 18, esp. pp. 306–13.

42. See *Phaedrus* 244–256, esp. 250–6. See further Price, *Love and Friendship*, ch. 3; G. R. F. Ferrari, *Listening to the Cicadas: A Study of Plato's* Phaedrus (Cambridge, 1987), ch. 6; C. J. Rowe, 'Philosophy, Love, and Madness', in C. Gill, ed., *The Person and the Human Mind* (Oxford, 1990), pp. 227–46.

43. For the role of the guide in the ascent, see *Smp.* 210a, c, e, 211c; for Diotima's guidance, see esp. 208b–c, 210a, 211d; for Socrates' consequential advice to the others, see 212b.

44. See further Gill, *Personality*, 5.3 and 5.7.

45. It is important to mark the distinction between these three stages in Aristotle's argument about

friendship: (1) describing conventional ideas, *NE* 8. 1–2; (2) formulating an ideal model of friendship, *NE* 8. 3–5; (3) analysing issue which arise in connection with this ideal, *NE* 9. 4, 8, 9. The equivalent stages in the other main ethical treatise, *Eudemian Ethics* (*EE*) are 7. 1; 7. 2; 7. 6, 12. On the structure of Aristotle's argument in both treatises, see Price, *Love and Friendship*, ch. 4, esp. pp. 103–8, and ch. 5.

46. For this type of criticism of Aristotle's approach, see e.g. W. D. Ross, *Aristotle* (London, 1923), p. 208. This type of criticism is noted, but not endorsed, by Williams, in *Ethics and the Limits of Philosophy*, pp. 35, 50–2.

47. See e.g. J. M. Cooper, 'Aristotle on Friendship', in A. O. Rorty, ed., *Essays on Aristotle's* Ethics (Berkeley, 1980), pp. 301–40, esp. pp. 332–4; J. Annas, 'Plato and Aristotle on Friendship and Altruism', *Mind* 86 (1977), 532–54; Kahn, 'Aristotle and Altruism'; R. Kraut, *Aristotle on the Human Good*, ch. 2; Irwin, *Aristotle's First Principles*, chs. 17–18.

48. Annas, *The Morality of Happiness*, pp. 249–62, esp. pp. 260–2; Annas contrasts this idea with the Stoic view that the motivation to benefit oneself and to benefit others are distinct but (both) primary types of motivation, pp. 262–76. See also her illuminating account of two later accounts of ethical development which try to combine, in different ways, the Aristotelian and Stoic approaches (pp. 276–87).

49. See e.g. Arist. *NE* 9. 4, 1166a2–9; also 8. 8, 1159a28–33: Aristotle's example of the loving mother, arguably, presupposes the norm of the mutually benefiting shared life (cf. Euripides, *Medea* 1024–7, 1029–35) which is not available in the case that Aristotle cites.

50. See *NE* 8. 3–5, esp. 1156b12–17, 1157b33–6; *EE* 7. 2, esp. 1236a14–15, 1236b3–6. The importance in Aristotle's account of the ideas of 'the shared life' and of reciprocation of well-wishing (*antiphilēsis, antiphilia*) is brought out by Price, *Love and Friendship*, pp. 118–19, 138–48; N. Sherman, *The Fabric of Character: Aristotle's Theory of Virtue* (Oxford, 1989), ch. 4, esp. pp. 132–6.

51. This line of thought is particulary clear in *NE* 9. 8, esp. 1168a18–1169b2, in which the link with the heroic ideal of cooperative honour is evident; on the heroic ideal, see text to nn. 10–17 above. See further Gill, *Personality*, 5. 4–5; and 'Altruism or Reciprocity in Greek Ethical Philosophy?', in Gill, Postlethwaite, and Seaford, edd., *Reciprocity in Ancient Greece* (forthcoming). These comments are intended as qualification of the view of the scholarly works cited in n. 47 above; Annas, ref. in n. 48 above, raises separate issues which I shall discuss elsewhere.

52. See A. A. Long and D. N. Sedley, *The Hellenistic Philosophers*, 2 vols. (Cambridge, 1987) (=LS): 22 F(2), Q(5) and (6), also G, H; numbers refer to sections, letters and bracketed numbers to ancient passages within sections.

53. See LS 21 E(2), also 21 A-B, O-P. 'Pleasure', for Epicurus, is defined as the absence of physical pain (*aponia*) and the absence of psychological disturbance (*ataraxia*).

54. See LS 22 E, F, I, O esp. (3), taken with the commentary in LS, vol. 1, pp. 137–8.

55. See LS 22 O(3) = Cicero, *De Finibus* (*Fin.*) 1. 67. See further P. Mitsis, *Epicurus' Ethical Theory: The Pleasures of Invulnerability* (Ithaca, 1988), ch. 3, esp. pp. 98–104, 112–17; Annas, *The Morality of Happiness*, pp. 236–44, esp. 239–40. The line of thought ascribed to Epicurus is similar to that ascribed to Aristotle, as a way of reconciling the pursuit of one's own happiness with the valuation of altruistic friendship; see refs. in n. 47 above.

56. Mitsis frames the issue in these terms and reaches this conclusion; *Epicurus' Ethical Theory*, pp. 123–8; cf. Annas's differently conceived, but similarly negative, conclusion, *The Morality of Happiness*, pp. 240–4.

57. LS 22 F(6–7), also 22 C(2), and 24 D–E.

58. For these two conditions, as reconciled in the ideal Epicurean friendship, see text to nn. 54–5 above. See further Gill, *Personality*, 5.7.

59. See e.g. *Republic* (*R.*) 519c8–d7, e4, 520a8–9, c1, e2, 521b7–10; also 499b5, 500d4.

60. On this role, see *R.* 520b5–c6; also 412c–e, 428a–429a, 433a–c.

61. *R.* 520d6–8, also b3–4.

62. On the basic argument in *R.* (and on the question whether it is coherently carried through), see e.g. J. Annas, *An Introduction to Plato's* Republic (Oxford, 1981), chs. 3, 6, 12–13; R. Kraut, 'The Defense of Justice in Plato's *Republic*', in Kraut, ed., *The Cambridge Companion in Plato* (Cambridge, 1992), pp. 311–37.

63. See Irwin, *Plato's Moral Theory*, pp. 242–3, also 233–41; a similar, but more moderately stated, view, is offered in *Plato's Ethics*, pp. 298–317, esp. 298–301, 313–16. For other responses to this problem see Annas, *Introduction in Plato's* Republic, pp. 266–71; C. D. C. Reeve, *Philosopher-Kings: The Argument of Plato's* Republic (Princeton, 1988), pp. 199–203.

64. On this role, and on the idea of 'justice' involved, i.e. 'doing your job', see refs in n. 60 above.

65. The latter point is highlighted in *R.* 519c–520a, 520d2–7, e4–521a4. It partly explains the language of 'compulsion' (refs. in n. 59 above); a further (partial) explanation for the use of such language is that the logic of Plato's argument requires (or 'compels') the philosopher-rulers to act in this way: see 519c9–10, 520a8, 521b7, 520d3.

66. See e.g. *Il.* 12. 310–28; see also text to nn. 14–17 above.

67. The two stages are described in Books 2–3 and 6–7 of *R.* respectively. On the idea of the 'internalization' of values (in heroic ethics), see text to nn. 24–5 above; on Plato's tripartite psyche, and the process of making this 'reason-ruled', see Ch. II, text to nn. 27–31.

68. See *R.* 500b–501b (also 498e), taken with 400d–402c, esp. 402a–c; also 519b–520c.

69. See *R.* 485d–e, contrasted with the pre-reflective *sōphrosunē* of 430e–432a, 442a, c–d, also 402c–403c. See also the philosopher's courage, based on knowledge of 'all time and all reality' (486a–b), contrasted with the pre-reflective (citizen's) courage of 429b–430c.

70. *R.* 580–7, esp. 581b, 582b–d, 585c–586b.

71. See further Gill, *Personality*, 4.6.

72. For reviews of the debate, see Kraut, *Aristotle and the Human Good*, pp. 7–9 and ch. 5; A. Kenny, *Aristotle on the Perfect Life* (Oxford, 1992), pp. 4–42, 86–93. In Rorty, *Essays on Aristotle's* Ethics, chs. 1–2, 18–20 relate to this question.

73. See e.g. Nussbaum, *Fragility of Goodness*, pp. 373–8; K. V. Wilkes, 'The Good Man and the Good for Man in Aristotle's Ethics', in Rorty, *Essays on Aristotle's* Ethics, pp. 341–57.

74. Key relevant passages are *NE* 1. 7, 1098a16–18; 6. 7, esp. 1141a18–b12; 6. 12, esp. 1144a1–6; 6. 13, esp. 1145a6–11; also *Metaphysics* 12. 7, 9, taken with *NE* 10.7, 1177b26–1178a22. For this view, see e.g. Kraut, *Aristotle on the Human Good*; J. Lear, *Aristotle: The Desire to Understand* (Oxford, 1988), esp. chs. 1, 4, and 6. 8. A further issue is whether *EE* holds the same view on this matter as *NE*. Kenny takes *EE* to present an inclusive conception of happiness, *Aristotle on the Perfect Life*, pp. 93–102. But the crucial passage at the end of *EE* 8. 3, 1249b6–25, is interpreted by M. Woods as expressing a dominant conception; see *Aristotle*: Eudemian Ethics *I, II, and VIII*, tr. with commentary (Oxford, 1992, 2nd edn.), pp. 180–4. On the relationship between *EE* and *NE*, in general, see Kenny, *The Aristotelian Ethics* (Oxford, 1978).

75. Kraut, *Aristotle on the Human Good*, ch. 2, esp. pp. 78–86; for a different view, see text to nn. 49–51 above.

76. *NE* 10. 8, 1178b5–6, taken with 1178a9–22. See Kraut, *Aristotle on the Human Good*, pp. 177–82, 188–9, 341–53; also Kenny, *Aristotle on the Perfect Life*,. pp. 90–1, 105.

77. Kraut, *Aristotle on the Human Good*, pp. 59–60 and ch. 6, esp. pp. 341–5; also pp. 74, 170–8, 182–4.

78. See text to nn. 43–4 above.

79. S. Broadie, *Ethics with Aristotle* (New York, 1991), pp. 392–8. In general, Aristotle states that a practical understanding of ethical virtue is a prerequisite of worthwhile ethical enquiry. See *NE* 1. 3–4, 10. 9, esp. 1179b4–29, taken with M. Burnyeat, 'Aristotle on Learning to be Good', in Rorty, ed. *Essays on Aristotle's* Ethics, pp. 69–92, esp. pp. 75–81. Aristotle's own surviving treatises are based on lectures in his school to students and fellow-philosophers whom he, presumably, regarded as meeting these requirements.

80. See 10. 7, 1177b30–1, 1178a2–4, taken with 9. 4, 1166a13–23, 9. 8, 1168b34–1169a2. For this suggestion, see Gill, *Personality*, 5.7. On the form of argument in *NE* 10. 7–8, see also Ch. V, text to nn. 69–72.

81. Thus, this interpretation fits in with an ethical framework which regards mutual benefit rather than altruism as the norm of interpersonal ethics, and which conceives the motive to benefit others in the light of this norm.

82. See esp. text to nn. 21–9 above.

83. See nn. 1 and 37 above; I take it that this framework provides the explanatory context for the (complex) ethical cases considered in this section; see esp. text to nn. 64–6, 78–81 above.

IV. INDIVIDUALS IN COMMUNITIES

1. *Greek and Modern Political Concepts*

Although there has been a good deal of important new work on Greek political philosophy, there has not, until recently, been the same intensity or volume of scholarly debate as in the case of Greek ethical philosophy;[1] and it would not be so easy to define prevalent trends. I offer, instead, a personal treatment of one important strand in Greek political theory, which both draws on some recent scholarly thinking and complements the themes of other chapters in this book.

In modern political philosophy, a dominant contrast has been that between the 'individual' and 'society' or the 'state'. This has served both as a way of formulating political ideals (such as 'individualism' or 'socialism'), and of defining the central issues in political theory, whether or not this is written from a particular political standpoint. It is easy for us to treat this contrast a providing a universal framework for analysing the political thinking of other eras and cultures. But, in fact, the prevalence of this contrast seems to go back no further than the seventeenth century, and it is often used in a way that specifically reflects Western political life in the late nineteenth and early twentieth centuries. The idea that the individual should be treated as an economic or moral unit can be traced back to Hobbes or Locke, or, in another way, to Rousseau and Kant. 'Individualism', as some recent books have underlined, has become a complex and many-layered ideal, with political, ethical, and psychological aspects.[2] The notion of the 'state', in early modern thinking, tends to be centred on the role of the monarch and his ministers. From the nineteenth century, however, it has been associated with the political institutions of national or supra-national states. Since Marx and Engels, 'socialism' and 'society' have come to represent ethical and political ideals or concepts which are defined by contrast with 'individualism' and the 'individual'.

Although Greek thought is sometimes interpreted in terms of this type of contrast,[3] it is one which, arguably, fails to correspond to Greek concepts or issues. The idea of the 'individual' has no clear equivalent in the Greek language; one has to choose between the general category of 'human being' (*anthrōpos*) and more determinate social roles, such as 'citizen', 'mother', 'friend'.[4] *Polis* is, after the Homeric period, the obvious candidate for 'state' or 'society'; but the forms of political life maintained in these small, integrated units is very different from that in modern nation-states or superpowers and is one that lends itself much less well to analysis in terms of the contrast between 'individual' and 'state'. Broadly speaking, Greek social and political life (and these two modes of Greek life are not easy to separate from each other) take the form of (differing kinds and degrees of) participation in a nexus of overlapping forms of relationship. These relationships include those of the family, friendship-group or symposiastic circle, village, neighbourhood, or deme, as well as those which derive (for citizens) from participation in the *polis* and in trading and social ties with those outside the *polis*. Given this situation, it is unsurprising that Greek political theory gives so much attention to subjects, such as education, family-upbringing, and the arts, that are not typically considered as 'political' in modern theory, or that Greek political theory overlaps significantly with ethical theory.[5] It is also unsurprising that, even in democratic Athens of the fifth-fourth centuries, in which participation in the institutions of the *polis* was most widely shared, at least among adult males, political ideals interlock (or are in tension) with ideals of family solidarity or of reciprocity which derive from non-political forms of social life.[6]

When this characteristic of Greek political thought has been noticed (it has not always been), scholars have tended to contrast Greek thinking in this respect with modern political thought and life. However, a recent feature of political life, especially in the UK and USA, is that some people have called into question the modern practice of framing issues in terms of the contrast between 'individualism' and 'socialism', or between the 'individual' and the 'state'. There has been much discussion of the importance of the role of 'communities' (including families, neighbourhoods, and other small-scale social groups) in providing intermediate structures, which form contexts for shared responsibility and mutual benefit. These ideas have come both from the political right and left (that is, roughly, from the 'individualist' and 'socialist' sides of the debate); and they have been linked with strands in recent ethical and sociological, as well as political, theory.[7] Against this background, the prevalent Greek patterns of thinking take on a special interest.[8] 'Individuals' (in so far as this is a relevant notion in the Greek context) function within 'communities' of this complex, overlapping type; and 'political' theory presupposes this background.

A related point is this. Much modern political thinking (both practical and theoretical) has centred on the idea that political life should be shaped by certain general ideals: these include liberty, equality, fraternity, the right to life, liberty, and the pursuit of happiness, or 'human rights'. Greek thinking also contains the idea that political life should express certain general human goods or virtues. But it also contains, I think, a much more fully worked-out picture of the way in which these ideals need to be embedded in the structures of relationship that make up social and 'political' life, in the broadest sense, and that shape the development of human character and ways of thinking. This too is an area where modern thought has, arguably, a good deal to learn from Greek thought.[9]

In this chapter, I pursue these points in two ways. First, I consider a number of cases, from Homer's Achilles onwards, in which it *might* seem, and has seemed to some scholars, that the 'individual', in a relatively strong sense, is conceived as a locus of meaning and value separate from the community in which he participates. I suggest, by contrast, that the relevant figure is better understood as appealing to the best principles of his community, as he understands these, in complaint against what he sees as breaches in the maintenance of these principles. (In my third case, that of Plato's Socrates, the issue is complicated by the fact that the best principles of the *polis* seem to be conceived as being those which apply universally to human beings.[10]) This topic overlaps with the second one: that of the ideal of the 'virtuous community'. Greek political theory typically takes the form of defining an ideal community, in which the totality of relationships, and not simply 'political' functions, are shaped by the best principles of the community. I distinguish three versions of this idea: (1) that in which the excellence of the community inheres simply in the coordination of its socio-political functions; (2) that in which there is a person or group in the community which also understands these principles; (3) that in which *all* participant members of the community have this understanding. (These versions are, broadly speaking, those of Aristotle's *Politics*; Plato's *Republic*, *Politicus*, and *Laws*; and the Stoic and Epicurean communities of 'the wise', respectively.[11]) A general point, applying to all three versions, is that they are not well analysed in terms of the relationship between the 'individual' and 'society'. A further general point is that, although these ideals are sometimes presented as being in sharp contrast to the socio-political life in the thinker's own *polis*, they are not 'individualist' ideals either as constituting a purely personal rejection of social norms or as constituting an ideal context for the expression of individualism. Rather, they represent attempts to describe the types of communal context (the nexus of forms of relationship) in which human beings as such (not 'individuals', in any strong sense) can live the best possible life.

2. *Individuals Against the Community?*

My first example of a case where a figure has been thought to take up an individualistic stance towards his community is that of Homer's Achilles, who rejects in *Il.* 9 the gifts offered by Agamemnon to compensate for his insult in seizing Achilles' prize-bride. Achilles' rejection of the gifts is sometimes though to constitute a complete negation of the ethics of his community, and an appeal to some form of individually conceived ethic. For Cedric Whitman, for instance, 'Achilles activated the absolute in the terms in which he had conceived it for himself ... The absolute is the ability and right of the heroic individual to perceive – or better, to conceive – law for himself, and then prove his case by action' (*Homer and the Heroic Tradition* (Cambridge, Mass., 1958), p. 213). Adam Parry, in a famous article on 'the language of Achilles', suggested that certain key questions and demands in Achilles' great speech (*Il.* 9. 308–429) represent an abuse of Homeric language by someone who is disillusioned with the ethics of his community but who has no other form of ethical language with which to express his disillusionment.[12] Parry's article has generated extensive debate about whether Achilles' speech does, indeed, constitute an abuse of Homeric language and a rejection of his community's ethics.[13] In one of the most valuable contributions to this debate, Richard Martin has shown that Achilles' great speech is, indeed, non-standard and relatively un-formulaic in its use of Homeric language, but also that it makes a coherent and intelligible statement through this unusual language.[14]

Recent work on the role of the idea of reciprocity in Homeric ethics can help us to see both why one might regard Achilles' rejection of the gifts as amounting to a rejection of his community's ethics, and also why this interpretation may not be, after all, the most convincing one. Achilles' great speech is often contrasted with Sarpedon's in *Il.* 12. 310–28. The latter speech can be seen as expressing the relationship of 'generalized' reciprocity, in which one party (the chieftain or hero) risks his life in battle in return for the honour and respect (*timē*) conferred by his people or fellow-chieftain. Honour is expressed especially in appropriate forms of gift-of-honour (*geras*) during life and in fame after death.[15] On the face of it, Achilles' speech rejects the validity of this type of reciprocal pattern.[16] Achilles is also non-standard in his refusal to accept the 'compensatory' reciprocity embodied in Agamemnon's gifts (378–87), despite the fact that, as Ajax points out later (632–8), it is normal to do so even in the case of more serious offences, such as murder of kin.[17]

However, reference to the ethics of reciprocity can also help us to see why Achilles might see his rejection of the gifts as justified. His speech can be interpreted as stating, or implying, several interrelated points relating to this ethical framework. The central thought is that Agamemnon's seizure of Achilles' prize-bride has been so unjustified, and so out of line with normal patterns of reciprocity between chieftains, that Agamemnon cannot now be treated as an acceptable donor of compensatory gifts. The offence caused is the greater, Achilles suggests, because of Achilles' own past willingness to participate fully in reciprocal comradeship, risking his life unsparingly in response to the Trojans' seizure of Helen.[18] A related point, implied in Achilles' way of rejecting the compensatory gifts, is that the very scale and magnificence of Agamemnon's gifts (combined with the way that they have been offered) constitute an attempt to reassert his authority over Achilles by gaining the added status that comes from superiority in gift-giving.[19] Finally, Agamemnon's attempted reassertion of authority, following his heavy-handed seizure of the prize-bride, are presented, by implication, as negating the chieftain's right to perform acts of reciprocation as generous gestures (or acts of favour, *charis*) rather than under pressure or coercion.[20]

Achilles' bitter, ironic comments and questions (especially 371–20, 337–9, 406–16), in which he seems to call into question the ethics of reciprocal comradeship, need to be taken in the context of his overall argument. In essence, his point is that, *under these circumstances*, in which Agamemnon fails to conduct properly the procedures of reciprocity, it is not worthwhile for anyone (especially him) to participate in them.[21] But the explicit appeal in his speech to proper standards of reciprocity implies that he would think it right to do so under other circumstances and with more ethically acceptable partners.[22] As I have suggested elsewhere, his rejection of the gifts can be taken, not so much as a complete rejection of the communal ethical framework but rather as an 'exemplary gesture'. It is designed to signal what he sees as fundamental breaches in the maintenance of this framework, even at the cost of performing an act that is non-standard by reference to this framework. As with other such gestures, Achilles' gesture is accompanied by, and rests on, reflective thought about the nature and basis of this ethical framework, implied in the bitter generalizations that he makes in the course of his speech. These generalizations, taken in context, can be interpreted as articulating the conception of a human life implied in this ethical framework rather than denying its validity.[23]

Another example in Greek poetry that can be analysed in broadly similar terms is the decision of Sophocles' Ajax to kill himself, following his failed attempt to take revenge on Odysseus and the Atreidae for not awarding him the arms of Achilles. Ajax's stance in this play is sometimes interpreted as a type of heroic individualism that takes little or no account of cooperative ethics, either as regards his comrades or his family. For instance, Mary Whitlock Blundell describes Ajax as 'rejecting the values of others without confronting them or engaging them in argument, which would undermine his self-sufficient isolation'; while R. P. Winnington-Ingram sees his speeches as marked by a type of heroism that amounts to 'megalomaniac pride'.[24] However, even the scholars who use this kind of interpretative language do not have in view the kind of *radical* individualism, and the negation of all communal ethics, that has been a feature of some modern thinking.[25] What they have in mind is, rather, the maintenance of the ethics of shame and honour in an excessively individualistic way, which takes no account of the opinions of Ajax's fellow-chieftains or of the claims of his wife and children, who will be left defenceless by his suicide.[26]

However, in this case too, I think it may be helpful to see Ajax's suicide as an 'exemplary gesture', designed to dramatize what Ajax sees as a fundamental breach in comradely ethics. What provoked his attack on his former comrades is not just the humiliation of not being awarded the arms, but also the *unjustified* nature of this humiliation, a point indicated in these crucial lines:

> ... if Achilles were alive and in the position of deciding about the arms, no one else would have obtained them rather than me. But, as things are, the Atreidae secured them for a man of unscrupulous character, dismissing my achievements in war. [If madness had not prevented my revenge] ... they would never have given judgement in this way on another man.[27]

Ajax can be seen, like Achilles in *Il.* 9, as having tried to respond, with reciprocal violence, to a fundamental breach in comradely reciprocity.[28] It is his failure to take what he sees as a justified revenge for this breach that makes it imperative for him to make the exemplary gesture of 'dying nobly', since he is unable to live nobly.[29] It is, arguably, this imperative that prevents Ajax from making any explicit reply to the counter-claim of his wife Tecmessa that nobility require him to stay alive to defend his family.[30] There is no coherent way in which Ajax can both respond effectively to her claim and to that of the exemplary gesture that he feels he must make.

However, it is possible to see the later 'deception-speech' (646–92), as containing an implied response to her claim, especially if, like some recent accounts, we see the speech as an oblique statement of Ajax's reasons for maintaining his decision, rather than as an attempt to deceive his *philoi* about the nature of his decision.[31] As well as expressing his pity at the thought of his wife and child being left without his support (652–3), he also conveys, in bitter, ironic mode, what it would mean for him to meet her request to change his mind and remain alive to protect them. He would need to have become 'womanized in his speech' (651), and to have learnt the kind of 'self-control' (*sōphronein*) that makes one 'yield to the gods and worship (*sebein*) the Atreidae' (666–8, 677). He would also have had to accept that there is no firm basis for reciprocal friendship (678–83). The latter comment especially confirms the suggestion made earlier, that Ajax sees the failure of the Greek leaders to award him the arms as a massive breach in reciprocal comradeship. After the failure of his attempt to avenge that offence, there is no appropriate gesture that he can make except suicide (especially as continued life would require the kind of humiliating self-abasement indicated in his speech).[32] On this interpretation, Ajax, like Achilles in *Il.* 9, sees his attack and his suicide, problematic though these are, as grounded on reflection on the implications of the ethics of comradely reciprocity. He sees the claims of his gesture as overriding those of the defence of his family, but he does not, on this view, ignore these.[33]

My third example of a figure who seems to take up an individualistic stance towards his community (but whose stance can be interpreted differently) is that of Socrates. The case of Socrates raises fundamental difficulties both about what counts as relevant evidence and about how this evidence should be interpreted. Like most recent accounts, I focus on the picture of Socrates given in the early Platonic dialogues. I do so not because I share the confidence of some recent accounts that the early Platonic dialogues provide a reliable and representative picture of the historical Socrates.[34] Socrates was, evidently, a hugely controversial figure in his own time, both politically and intellectually; and all our evidence, including Plato's, is more or less explicitly coloured by the author's aims, interests, and sympathies. The difficulty of obtaining from such sources an objective account of the historical Socrates (if this is a reasonable goal) remains formidable.[35] I focus on the early Platonic evidence because this represents a (broadly) consistent picture of the methods and arguments of Socrates, and one which has been deeply influential in antiquity as well as in modern times.[36] I think that Plato's Socrates can be seen as playing a crucial role in the history of Greek thinking about the relationship between the individual and community in two principal ways, both of which are implied by his method and arguments rather than stated explicitly. One of these is that the principles guiding action in any one community should be those which can be justified rationally (the implication is that they should be universally valid). The other is that, for every member of the community, ethical beliefs should be based on reflective debate or dialectic rather than on the internalization of communal beliefs.

There are two principal ways of analysing Socrates' position on the relationship between the individual and the community. One relates to his attitude towards the ethical and political life of Athens; the other relates to the respective roles of individual and community in determining ethical principles. One point of access to the first topic is provided by an apparent contradiction between Socrates' stance towards Athenian law in the *Apology* and in the *Crito*. In the *Apology*, Socrates claims that he would continue with his 'divine' mission of engaging Athenians in dialectical questioning, even if the court acquitted him on the condition that he stopped doing so (29c–e). In the *Crito*, Socrates bases his refusal to try to escape from prison (as he is urged to do by Crito) on the grounds that, by remaining a citizen of Athens, he has made a 'contract' with the laws of the city to obey their commands, whatever these are (50a–54c, esp. 51b–c, 52c–d). There is, on the face of it, a substantive philosophical conflict between these two positions. Can these positions be reconciled with each other? The contradiction is not one, I think, that can be removed simply by drawing a distinction between rejecting the offer of a conditional discharge and disobeying a law, or between the legal status of a localized court decision and a well-established law. Nor is it removed by the fact that the conditional discharge considered in the *Apology* is a purely hypothetical one.[37] Rather more significant is the distinction between the covert evasion of the law envisaged in the *Crito* and the public, principled defiance of it (the 'civil disobedience') envisaged in the *Apology*.[38] However, I think that the most suggestive approach to this question is that of Richard Kraut, who emphasizes that the *Crito* imagines the Laws of Athens as requiring its citizens to obey 'or to persuade them in accordance with the nature of justice' ($\pi\epsilon\iota\theta\epsilon\iota\nu$ . . . $\mathring{\eta}$ $\tau\grave{o}$ $\delta\iota\kappa\alpha\iota o\nu$ $\pi\acute{\epsilon}\phi\upsilon\kappa\epsilon$). Kraut thinks that Socrates' announcement of his principled rejection of a conditional discharge in the *Apology* could be classified as this type of (attempted) 'persuasion'. Even if Socrates failed to persuade, the attempt to persuade on these ground could be seen as providing a justification for Socrates' continued practice of dialectic, even if he had been acquitted on the condition that he stopped practising dialectic.[39]

There is, of course, room for argument about the success of Kraut's attempt to reconcile these two positions, and, more generally, about how far we *should* try to reconcile the positions taken up in the course of different Platonic dialogues, even ones apparently written in the same period.[40] However, discussion of this question highlights two important general features of Socrates' thinking, as presented in Plato's early dialogues. One is that Socrates' position is not credibly described a 'individualistic', if this implies the attempt to establish an ethical or political position which is wholly independent of the beliefs and practices current in his community (that is, the Athens of his day). On the other hand, it is also clear that Socrates' position rests on much more than the straightforward adoption of those beliefs and practices. Both Socrates' maintenance of his 'divine' mission and his assertion of the wrongness of trying to escape from prison (whether or not these two assertions are consistent with each other) depend on a reasoned, reflective response to the ethical and political beliefs and practices of Athenian communal life.[41] In the case of the heroic figures (Achilles, Ajax), considered earlier, I have suggested that certain crises in their relationship to their community stimulate them to an unusual degree of reflectiveness, though one that is still based on their communal ethical framework.[42] However, Socrates' position differs from these heroic ones in two respects. For one thing, a clear implication of Socrates' mission (that of engaging each member of his community in dialectical enquiry about fundamental ethical questions) is that *everyone* should base his actions on such reasoned reflection, and not just exceptional people in exceptional situations. Secondly, there is at least an implied demand that such reflection should seek to determine universally valid ethical norms, whether or not these coincide with those current in the relevant community at the relevant time.[43]

The latter point also emerges from current debate about the objectives and the truth-status of Socratic dialectic as depicted in the early Platonic dialogues. Gregory Vlastos, in stressing the centrality of Socrates' method of logical cross-examination (*elenchos*), also stresses a profound tension or contradiction that arises from Socrates' presentation of this method. On the one hand, Socrates presents the method as drawing on the beliefs of the interlocutors and as reaching conclusions which depend on the agreement of the interlocutors. On the other hand, he presents the goal of the discussion as (unqualified and universal) knowledge of truth, and he seems sometimes to imply that the argument has reached true conclusions. What justifies Socrates' confidence that truth can be achieved in this way and (sometimes) that it has been achieved? As Vlastos sees the matter, there must be certain beliefs (those which tend to recur in Socrates' arguments and are sometimes called his 'paradoxes') which can be known to be true because they survive repeated examination in argument.[44] Charles Kahn, developing this line of thought in connection with Plato's *Gorgias*, shows how Socrates may reasonably think that argument directed at showing the inconsistencies in the positions of particular people may, none the less, yield objective truth. Socratic dialectic does so by eliciting even from misguided and uncooperative interlocutors *enough* true beliefs (beliefs consistent with Socrates' set of unrefutable beliefs) to guarantee that the false beliefs of these interlocutors are shown to be inconsistent with these true beliefs.[45]

There is scope for argument about whether Vlastos's description of Socratic dialectic and the resolution of the problem that he offers are credible or coherent.[46] But, leaving aside the more controversial parts of his interpretation, Vlastos's account brings out the point noted earlier, that Socratic dialectic requires each interlocutor to reflect about his action-guiding principles. It also suggests that the objective of dialectic is to establish principles that are universally valid, whether or not they are also regarded as valid in the interlocutor's own community. Socrates' position can be defined by contrast with that attributed to one of the best-known sophists, Protagoras, in Plato's dialogue of that name. In his great speech, Protagoras, first of all, offers a 'utilitarian' account of ethics: that 'shame' (*aidōs*) and 'justice' (*dikē*) emerged in human society because of the need for communal cohesion to enable human beings to survive destruction at the hands of stronger animals (322b–c). He also offers a communal or communitarian account of ethical eduction: children and adults acquire virtue by 'internalizing' the ethical beliefs current in their communities.[47]

Protagoras' speech may also imply a version of the relativism which is, in various forms, ascribed to him by ancient sources, namely the idea that each type of community (e.g. the democratic) develops the conception of shame and justice that suits its general character.[48] The position implied in Socrates' method and arguments can be contrasted with Protagoras' in that, for Socrates, ethical development depends on dialectical reflection, and the ethical standards established in this way must be universal or objective ones. As I bring out in the next section, the interplay between the Socratic position and the more communitarian one exemplified by Protagoras can be seen as constituting an important feature of subsequent Greek thinking about the best form of community.

3. *The Virtuous Community*

The points made in the previous section, especially those relating to Plato's Socrates, provide relevant background for my second main topic, that of the thinking about individual and community in Greek political theory from Plato to the Stoics. As explained in Section 1, I do not think that Greek thinking of this type lends itself to analysis in terms of the contrast between 'individual' and 'state' or 'society', or of the ideals ('individualism' or 'autonomy', on the one hand, or 'socialism' or 'collectivism', on the other) often associated with this contrast. Greek thinking expresses a conception of life as normally lived in and through forms of community. The *polis* is, typically, regarded as providing the best possible framework for these forms of communal life; and reflection about the merits of different types of constitution (*politeia*), that is, about different ways of organizing the *polis*, represents a central and characteristic feature of Greek political theory. But the *polis* is also seen as the context for a whole nexus of types of communal relationships (including those of family, friendship-group, deme or local town and so forth). Arguably, the most characteristic feature of Greek political theory (which is, thus 'political' in a broad sense) is debate about the best possible form of shared human life, and about the communal, educational, and artistic frameworks in which this can take place. It is no accident that the boundaries of Greek 'political' theory are not very clearly defined. For Plato, the Stoics, and Epicureans (in so far this is a relevant notion for them), political theory largely overlaps with ethical; and this is also true for Aristotle, even though he is the first (and perhaps only) Greek thinker to define these as separate, though linked, areas of enquiry.[49]

Although all these theories see communal life as a way of realizing (a certain conception of) the human good or happiness, the theories are not helpfully differentiated in this respect, since several theories share the same conception of this good, namely 'virtue', in some sense.[50] A more helpful criterion is one that derives from the interplay between communal and dialectical views of the nature and basis of ethical life and education discussed in connection with Socrates and Protagoras.[51] For Aristotle, a good *polis* is one whose organization and way of life enable it to realize human happiness, whether or not any one class of persons within the community has a dialectically-based understanding of human happiness and of the way that this is realized by the community. For Plato, in the *Republic*, and, to a lesser extent, the *Laws*, the *polis* cannot realize this objective unless its communal life is decisively shaped by a class of persons which does have this understanding. For the Stoics, at least in one strand of their (many-layered) thinking on this topic, and for the Epicureans, the only wholly worthwhile kind of community (which may not resemble conventional societies at all closely) is a community of 'the wise', who share this dialectically-based understanding.[52] In exploring this three-fold distinction,

I seek to bring out how these differences inform other features of the theories (such as their thinking about constitutional organization), and also how this gives rise to a pattern of thinking about shared human life that is very different from that associated in modern thought with the contrast between 'individual' and 'society'.

The latter point comes out clearly in connection with the first, and most famous, large-scale work of Greek theory about the best possible form of communal life, Plato's *Republic*. In the period after the Second World War, Plato's *Republic* and *Laws*, together with Aristotle's *Politics*, were taken by Karl Popper as prefiguring the political approach of totalitarianism, which, either in its Fascist or Communist form, subordinates the claims of the individual to those of the state. In the ensuing debate, scholars attacked or defended Plato and Aristotle by reference to modern political concepts and ideals.[53] Although the gap between the Greek material and the modern concepts used in this debate has become obvious, the question how far Plato's *Republic* leaves room for the exercise of individual autonomy (ethical or political) sometimes figures in recent discussions.[54] However, the *Republic* lends itself less well to this kind of analysis even than most Greek works of political theory. The *Republic* consists of a unique two-fold defence of the claim that justice constitutes happiness, conducted both on the individual (or rather psychological) level and on the political level.[55] This two-fold structure might seem, on the face of it, to correspond to the modern distinction between the individual and the state, and to provide the basis for argument about the respective claims of these. However, the implication of this combined psychological and political argument is, rather, to reinforce the general Greek view that individual human lives are realized in forms of community. More precisely, the *Republic* suggests that the ideal, or 'reason-ruled', *psuchē* can only develop fully in the 'reason-ruled' community, and that the existence of the 'reason-ruled' community depends on the existence of a class of persons who possess a 'reason-ruled' *psuchē*.[56]

At the heart of the *Republic*'s argument about justice is an account of the two-stage educational programme for the philosopher-rulers. This functions both as an account of the education of the ruling class (and, in effect, as a model of the relationship between rulers and ruled), and as a way of characterizing the nature and development of the ideal, 'reason-ruled' personality. As outlined in the preceding chapter, the first stage consists in the 'internalization' of correct communal beliefs and standards by the young guardians and the correlated shaping of aspirations and desires. The second stage provides the analytic understanding of those beliefs and standards and the basis for applying them in moulding the life of the community.[57] In presenting this programme, Plato lays great stress on the interdependence of the two stages. It is only dialectic based on the foundation of the pre-dialectical shaping of character and beliefs that can reliably lead to knowledge of objective ethical truths.[58] And it is only in a community governed by those with dialectically-based knowledge of these truths that communal life can provide this foundation.[59] It follows from this that individuals can only become fully just in a community which is itself already just, and which offers this kind of educational programme.[60] This raises in an acute form a problem which Plato does not avoid: that of whether the ideal state can ever come into existence, since such a state requires the prior existence of a class of persons (those fully equipped to be philosopher-rulers), who cannot exist without the prior existence of the ideal state's educational programme.[61] Although this represents a serious problem for anyone seeking to define the ethical and political implications of the *Republic*, it reinforces the principal point that I am making here. This is that his work embodies a way of thinking in which the 'individual' and the 'state' (or, better, the psychological and the communal lives of human beings) are inseparably linked, and in which their improvement and deterioration go hand in hand.[62]

The *Republic* also exhibits two further general features, which can be paralleled in other Platonic dialogues on political themes, and, to some extent, other works of Greek political theory. One is that (what modern readers tend to think of as) the more purely 'political' aspects of the work, the constitutional arrangements in the ideal state, are embedded in a larger study of human social (and psychological) life, including reference to education, music, drama, gymnastics, family- and gender-relationships.[63] In this respect, as in the one noted earlier in this chapter, the understanding of what count as the 'political' anticipates that of contemporary thinking, by contrast with more traditional conceptions of what 'politics' means in our culture.[64] The *Laws* goes even further in this direction, situating its constitutional arrangements in the larger context of a cradle-to-grave (or rather embryo-to-grave) programme of communal life. Virtually all aspects of normal Greek family and social life, including the symposium, religious rituals, the role of women in shaping ethical attitudes in family life, as well as the management of private property and political deliberation, are conceived as possible forms of participation in the virtuous community.[65] Although the constitution of the *Laws* is presented as 'second-best' to that of the *Republic* in not setting out to reform family life and the 'privatization' of interests and goals that goes along with family life, it is still firmly focussed on the idea that the life of the community as a whole should be directed at the realization of virtue (as a means of realizing human happiness).[66]

The second general feature of the *Republic*, which can be paralleled in other Platonic political works (and, to some extent, later Greek political theory) centres on the attitude towards conventional Greek constitutions. It is clear from texts such as the constitutional debate in Herodotus 3. 80–2, and Pericles' funeral speech in Thucydides 2. 37–41, that the standard types of Greek constitution (especially democracy, oligarchy, monarchy) were presented, by representatives of different standpoints, as effective ways of realizing the best possible form of communal life.[67] The *Republic* exhibits a studied detachment from political theorizing of this type. The *Republic* sets out to offer a generalized outline of what 'justice' means, in psychological and political terms, rather than a detailed blueprint even of an ideal constitution.[68] Although *Republic* 8–9 offers an ethical evaluation of different constitutional types, coupled with an examination of parallel psychological types, the relationship between these ethico-political types and normal Greek constitutions is not entirely clear. In the *Statesman* (or *Politicus*), the key political thesis is that the only real 'constitution' (*politeia*) is the kind of *polis* that is governed by a person or persons with objective ethical and political knowledge. The statesman's distinctive skill of 'weaving' together the political, social, and ethical life of the community is one that could be exercised, it would seem, in different types of constitution, and which does not depend on any specific constitutional framework for its effectiveness. It is only in the absence of such objective political skill that communities should rely on their traditional constitutional frameworks, which are preferable to the alternatives of lawlessness or the exercise of arbitrary power.[69] The *Laws* does outline in some detail a constitution, a type of 'hoplite democracy', with a limited number of property-owning citizens, an assembly, deliberative committee or *boulē*, elected magistrates, and a supervisory 'nocturnal council'.[70] But the core of the political theory of the *Laws* does not inhere in the specification of the constitutional structure, but rather in the shaping of the community as a whole, in all its functions, so as to constitute an ethically cohesive body.[71]

In terms of the threefold distinction between types of theory outlined earlier (text to n. 11), the *Republic* falls into the intermediate category, which combines communitarian and dialectical elements. The *Republic* requires *both* a community whose structure and shared life expresses right ('reason-ruled') beliefs *and* a ruling group (philosopher-rulers) which has a dialectically-based understanding of the truth and (normative) 'rationality' of those beliefs.[72] The *Statesman* also requires that the best type of community be shaped ('woven together') by a ruler or ruling group with objective political knowledge, but does not explicitly require that such knowledge be based on dialectical enquiry.[73] The *Laws* does specify the need for such dialectically-based knowledge, to be exercised by the 'nocturnal council', which has a special role in overseeing the working of the constitution (960–8). But, as some recent discussions have suggested, the main innovation in the political theory of the *Laws* lies elsewhere. What is most significant is the idea that the community should maximize the spread of true (and reasoned) ethical beliefs to the whole citizen body, and, as far as possible, the whole population, especially through the explanatory 'preludes' to the laws.[74] In this respect, the *Laws* can be seen as containing a theorized version of 'shame-ethics' (as interpreted in the preceding chapter), in which the community as a whole is encouraged to 'internalize' a set of ethical beliefs and not simply to respond to legal constraints and social pressures.[75]

Aristotle's *Politics* expresses explicitly the ideas that I have presented as characteristic of Greek political thought: that human beings are naturally adapted to form their lives through participation in communities, and that communities are the context through which human beings can achieve happiness through virtue. Aristotle famously, thinks that 'human beings are naturally adapted to live in a *polis*' (φύσει πολιτικὸν ὁ ἄνθρωπος), and that the *polis* is the best possible framework for a complete human life.[76] A *polis* is not just an institutional framework within which a (separately conceived) 'private' life occurs, but is, ideally, the context in which human beings can realize their happiness by virtuous participation in shared forms of life.[77] Aristotle's thinking is, in this respect, best understood neither as 'individualist' nor 'collectivist' but as 'participant' (that is, based on the assumption that human life is naturally expressed in participation in shared forms of life).[78]

In relation to the threefold distinction between types of theory drawn earlier, Aristotle defines the best type of community by reference to its constitutional structure and mode of life rather than by the possession of dialectically-based knowledge on the part of that ruling class.[79] However, he clearly believes that the kind of dialectical enquiry that constitutes political theory can, in principle, yield objective understanding of the goals of political structures, and that political theory is normative and not simply descriptive or analytic.[80] For instance, he not only discusses the standard types of constitutional forms in Greek life, but distinguishes between correct and incorrect versions of these, according to whether the rulers rule in their own interests or those of the community as a whole (3. 6–7). Also, while recognizing that 'justice' has a different meaning in different constitutions, he thinks that it is possible to define in general terms an objectively 'just' form of government, namely one in which participation in government corresponds with the virtue of the person concerned.[81] For related reasons, he does not endorse fully any of the standard forms of constitution in the Greek world, but identifies as the only real 'constitution' (*politeia*) one which exhibits *this* kind of 'justice' in its organization. Although justice may be found, to some extent, in any of the standard constitutional forms, he thinks that this is most likely to occur in a 'moderate' or 'mixed' constitution, a 'hoplite democracy' or 'moderate oligarchy' (4. 7–9). This preference resembles that of Plato's *Laws*;[82] indeed, in several ways, the *Politics* may be seen as offering a less Utopian version of Plato's *Laws*. For both thinkers, the best conceivable constitution is that which embodies the best possible understanding of human happiness and the fullest realization of this through the life-forms of the community, as well as through the form of government. Aristotle also thinks hat it is a function of the virtuous community to propagate ethical beliefs and emotional responses through education and artistic life.[83]

Aristotle's view that the community is right to propagate in this way its conception of virtue clearly creates unease in some modern scholars, who approach the question from the more liberal standpoint of modern democratic societies.[84] Another object of criticism has been Aristotle's readiness to provide a theoretical justification (by reference to the idea of what is 'natural') for the normal subordination of slaves and women in his culture, rather than highlighting the conventional character of these features, as Plato did. The latter point reflects a more general feature of his thought, namely his teleology or 'metaphysical biology'; and some recent accounts have tried to render Aristotle's views on natural rule more acceptable (or at least more intelligible) in the light of this feature.[85]

Plato's *Statesman* and *Laws*, and Aristotle's *Politics*, have been readily available for a long time, in editions and translations (though there have recently been some useful additions in this respect).[86] In the case of the political thought of the Stoics and Epicureans (as with other aspects of Hellenistic philosophy), the evidence is largely indirect, fragmentary, and difficult to interpret; but the upsurge of interest in Hellenistic philosophy has stimulated close attention to this topic too.[87]

In Stoic thinking, we can discern at least two main strands or phases, both of which centre on the idea of a 'community [or 'city'] of the wise'. The first, more radical strand is represented especially by Zeno's (lost)

Republic, a work which, like Plato's *Republic* (especially Book 5), advocated as 'natural' certain non-standard social practices such as the common possession of wives and incest.[88] The precise aim of this work is unclear: was it a Utopian programme for a possible state or a way of dramatizing general political ideals? But a key thought seems to be that the only real community is that which exists between the virtuous or wise; and that conventional communities (characterized by non-wise social and political institutions) are not communities in any real sense.[89] (I take it, though this is not wholly explicit, that a prerequisite of full wisdom or virtue is the kind of philosophical understanding of ethics and of what is 'natural' that is provided by Stoicism.)[90]

The second, more conventional, strand is represented by, for instance, Cicero, especially when drawing on the work of Panaetius (as, or instance, in *On Duties*). In this strand, by contrast, it is assumed that the social and political structures of conventional states constitute a framework in which people can practise the 'appropriate actions' (*kathēkonta*) that provide the means of development towards full virtue or wisdom.[91] A feature of Panaetius' thinking is the theory of the four roles (*personae*), which includes the idea that specific people should shape their lives in the light of what is appropriate to their specific talents and interests. But, taken in the context of the communal (and conventional) framework being presupposed, this idea does not lead to the more radical ethical individualism that we find in modern thinkers such as Nietzsche or Sartre.[92] In this strand of Stoic thinking (which can be found in a range of Hellenistic and Roman writers), ideas such as the 'community of the wise' or 'the city of gods and humans' figure (together with that of 'divine', or 'rational', 'law') as normative ideas. Such ideas are taken as providing an (objective and ultimate) framework on which to ground ethical life in conventional states, rather than as the basis for the rejection of conventional life, as they are for Zeno.[93] Both in the more radical and the more conventional strand of Stoicism we find the idea that the motivation to benefit others should go beyond family, friends, and city, to human beings as such. In the more radical strand, this forms part of the negation of conventional social and political structures. In the more conventional strand, it seems to represent again a normative ideal or horizon, which does not replace standard patterns of other-benefiting (or mutually benefiting) concern.[94]

The Epicureans do not, clearly, give such importance to communal life, and have sometimes been seen as radical individualists, as well as egoists. However, A. A. Long (with D. N. Sedley), in particular, has underlined that there are at least two important ways in which the Epicureans have a social or political philosophy. On the one hand, they have theories about the nature of justice in conventional (non-Epicurean) societies, namely that it is a 'social contract' or 'guarantee of utility', enabling people to live together in ordered communities.[95] (Lucretius' picture of the three-stage development of human civilization reflects this idea.[96]) On the other hand, in communities (such as has centred in Epicurus' own Garden) in which all the members lived by Epicurean ethical standards, laws would not be required to prevent wrongdoing: 'everything will be full of justice and mutual friendship, and there will be no need of city-walls and laws ...'[97] The claim is that a proper understanding of the nature of pleasure will bring with it the realization that, for instance, we can satisfy our physical needs with very little, a realization that brings with it the virtue of self-control (*sōphrosunē*).[98] As suggested earlier, crucial to the Epicurean theory of friendship (and virtue) is the idea that it is *Epicurean* (philosophically-based) standards of friendship or virtue that are involved, and a similar point applies to their theory of justice.[99] In this respect, the Epicureans, like the more radical strand of Stoic thought, take the view that the best kind of community (or, in a sense, the only real kind of community) depends on philosophically-based understanding.[100] Viewed in this light, the Epicureans have positive theories about the basis of an ideal community (as well as about the basis of communal life in conventional societies), and differ less from other Greek thinkers in this respect than is usually supposed.

NOTES

1. For instance, Aristotle's *Politics* (*Pol.*) has been less intensively discussed, until recently, than his ethical works (on which, see Ch. III, text to nn. 45–51, 72–81); for recent work on *Pol.*, see text to nn. 76–85 below. A partial exception is the post-war debate stemming from Popper's work (on which, see n. 53 below). An important book in preparation is the *Cambridge History of Ancient Political Thought*, edd. C. J. Rowe and M. Schofield (Cambridge, forthcoming).

2. See e.g. S. Lukes, *Individualism* (Oxford 1973); MacIntyre, *After Virtue* (London, 2nd edn. 1985), chs. 1–9; C. Taylor, *Sources of the Self: The Making of the Modern Identity* (Cambridge, 1989). On the partly parallel way in which the Cartesian ego (the unitary self-conscious 'I') became fundamental to the theory of mind, in a way that helped to shape subsequent thinking about the 'self', see Ch. II, text to nn. 7, 10.

3. See e.g. for debate about Pl. *R.*, considered as a work of political theory, text to nn. 53–4 below.

4. See further on this line of though M. Hollis, 'Of Masks and Men', in M. Carrithers, S. Collins, S. Lukes, edd., *The Category of the Person* (Cambridge, 1985), pp. 217–33.

5. This is a feature not just of Pl. *R.* or *Laws* (esp. 2. 6–7), but also Arist. *Pol.* (1. 7–8); see also the 'political' elements in *NE* 8. 9–11, 13–14, *EE* 7. 9–10, treated by Aristotle under the broad heading of 'friendship', *philia*. On the latter topic, see J. Cooper, 'Political Animals and Civic Friendship', with commentary by J. Annas, in G. Patzig, ed., *Aristoteles: Politik, Akten des XI Symposium Aristotelicum* (Göttingen, 1990), pp. 221–42.

6. See further G. Herman, 'Reciprocity, Altruism, and Exploitation: the Special Case of Classical Athens', and P. Millett, 'The Rhetoric of Reciprocity', both in Gill, Postlethwaite, and Seaford, edd., *Reciprocity in Ancient Greece* (Oxford, forthcoming). G. Hermann, *Ritualised Friendship and the Greek*

City (Cambridge, 1987), also discusses social and economic ties between members of different city-states.

7. Relevant political factors include the collapse of communism in the former USSR, and a reaction against the 'consumer' individualism of conservative governments in the UK and USA in the 1980's. On 'communitarianism', see e.g. A. Etzioni, *The Spirit of Community: Rights, Responsibilities and the Communitarian Agenda* (New York, 1994); *A Responsive Agenda* (New York, 1991). The work of A. MacIntyre, in *After Virtue* and other works, is an important influence on this way of thinking.

8. For a similar suggestion regarding modern responses to Aristotle, see the thoughtful introduction by R. F. Stalley to his revision of Ernest Barker's translation of Aristotle's *Politics* for World Classics (Oxford, 1995), pp. xxx–xxxii.

9. Modern 'identity-politics', centred on the idea that politics should be based on (e.g.) one's sexual (or gender) 'identity' might be seen as parallel to this feature of Greek thought, though Greek thought combines this feature with a stronger sense of the overall community (typically the *polis*) in which different types of relationship occur: see n. 64 below.

10. See text to nn. 43–5 below.

11. There is a partial overlap with the distinction between two types of ethical thinking outlined in Ch. III, text to n. 38; see further text to nn. 51–2 below.

12. A. Parry, 'The Language of Achilles', *TAPA* 87 (1956), 1–7; key relevant lines include *Il.* 9. 337–8, 387.

13. See e.g. M. D. Reeve, 'The Language of Achilles', *CQ* NS 23 (1973), 193–5; D. B. Claus, '*Aidos* in the Language of Achilles', *TAPA* 105 (1975), 13–28. J. M. Redfield, *Nature and Culture in the* Iliad*: The Tragedy of Hector* (Chicago, 1975), pp. 103–8, esp. 105, also sees the speech as expressing Achilles' alienation from his warrior-role, but does so on a different (largely structuralist) understanding of the nature of the role and of Achilles' alienation.

14. R. Martin, *The Language of Heroes: Speech and Performance in the* Iliad (Ithaca, 1989), pp. 160 ff. For instance, Martin shows that much of the speech is structured around the reasons that Achilles gives for 'not being persuaded' when you might expect him to be: see e.g. *Il.* 9. 315, 345, 376, 386, and Martin, pp. 202–3.

15. On 'generalized' and other forms of reciprocity in Homeric ethics, see Ch. III, text to n. 14.

16. See esp. *Il.* 9. 316–20, 337–9, 401–9.

17. R. A. S. Seaford, *Reciprocity and Ritual: Homer and Tragedy in the Developing City-State* (Oxford, 1994), pp. 65–73, esp. 69–70, treats the episode as a crisis in reciprocity, which is resolved at the level of ritual.

18. This interpretation assumes a connection between the rejection of the gifts in 9. 378–87 (and 388–97) and the complaints made in 315–43, esp. 334–41. The reiterated idea of 'not being persuaded' (see n. 14 above), in 315, 345, 375–6, 386, underlines the structure of Achilles' argument.

19. See 9. 378–400, esp. 391–2. Also, Agamemnon has not come in person to apologize (nor is his apology, such as it is, in 9. 115–20, passed on by Odysseus), nor made supplication (which Achilles might have looked for). Instead, he has sent Achilles' own *philoi* (9. 641–2) as his (Agamemnon's) agents. See further W. Donlan, 'Duelling with Gifts in the *Iliad*: As the Audience Saw It', *Colby Quarterly* 29 (1993), 155–72. See also, esp. on the absence of supplication, M. Edwards, *Homer: Poet of the* Iliad (Baltimore, 1987), pp. 233–4; A. Thornton, *Homer's* Iliad*: Its Composition and the Motif of Supplication* (Göttingen, 1984), pp. 126–7; O. Tsagarakis, 'The Achaean Embassy and the Wrath of Achilles', *Hermes* 99 (1971), 257–77, esp. pp. 259–63.

20. Note the stress on 'wishing' and absence of compulsion in 9. 356, 428–9, taken with Claus, '*Aidos* in the Language of Achilles'.

21. The point that Agamemnon's failure disqualifies him as a partner in reciprocal comradeship with *anyone*, not just Achilles, is implied in 9. 370–2, 417–20.

22. An indication of this is the fact that Achilles modifies his decision of 9. 357–63, in response to the speeches of Phoenix (9. 618–19), Ajax (9. 650–5), and, eventually, Patroclus (16. 64–100), i.e. partners with whom some form of comradely reciprocity is still possible, though it is no longer possible with Agamemnon.

23. See Ch. II, text to n. 25, on Medea's infanticide as an exemplary gesture, and see further C. Gill, *Personality in Greek Epic, Tragedy, and Philosophy*, 2. 4–8, esp. 2.8.

24. M. W. Blundell, *Helping Friends and Harming Enemies: A Study in Sophocles and Greek Ethics* (Cambridge,1989), p. 84; R. P. Winnington-Ingram, *Sophocles: An Interpretation* (Cambridge, 1980), pp. 47 (n. 109) and 41. See also B. M. W. Knox, *Word and Action* (Baltimore, 1979), pp. 12–14, 20–3;

and, on the conception of heroism presupposed, Knox, *The Heroic Temper: Studies in Sophoclean Tragedy* (Berkeley, 1965), ch. 1, esp. pp. 18–24.

25. For individualism of this radical kind (e.g. as expressed by Nietzsche or Sartre), see refs. in n. 2 above, esp. MacIntyre and Taylor.

26. See refs. in n. 24 above. Knox (and, in a modified way, Blundell) also sees Ajax's stance as the expression of an archaic ethical framework (the ethics of shame and honour), the limitations of which are highlighted by the more cooperative and (in some sense) 'developed' ethical attitudes of Odysseus, as expressed in lines 121–6, 1332–45.

27. Soph. *Ajax* 442–9; Odysseus, who was the one who received the arms, in effect endorses this claim, in describing Ajax as 'the best of the Achaeans . . . after Achilles' (1340–1); cf. Teucer's account of Ajax's acts of bravery, 1266–87, which he presents as deserving special gratitude (*charis*), 1267.

28. Like Achilles, Ajax can be interpreted as highlighting the kind of abuse of comradely behaviour that might emerge in the Atreidae's treatment of *any* of the Greek leaders; see text to nn. 21–3 above, esp. n. 21.

29. See Soph. *Ajax* 457–80; on the role of his father Telamon as the 'internalized other' before whom Ajax must prove his nobility, see 462–5, and B. Williams, *Shame and Necessity* (Berkeley, 1993), pp. 84–5, also 73–5; see Ch. III, text to n. 24. The gesture must also be directed at the Atreidae and Odysseus, whom he regards as objects of justified anger.

30. Soph. *Ajax* 485–524, esp. 522–4, in which Tecmessa appeals to the idea that favours merit reciprocal favours (χάρις χάριν . . .).

31. See e.g. Knox, *Word and Action*, pp. 135–44; Winnington-Ingram, *Sophocles*, pp. 54–5; Blundell, *Helping Friends and Harming Enemies*, pp. 84–5. For a different way of explaining the enigmatic character of the speech, by reference to mystery religion, see R. Seaford, 'Sophocles and the Mysteries', *Hermes* 122 (1994), 275–88, esp. pp. 282–4.

32. The attitude of the Atreidae (though not Odysseus) towards Ajax, as shown in 1067–9, 1087–8, 1250–4, bears out this picture of what would be required. The reversal of the expected phraseology in 666–8 ('yield to' the gods but '*worship*' the Atreidae) is evidently deliberate. On the significance of *sōphronein* in this play, see S. Goldhill, *Reading Greek Tragedy* (Cambridge, 1986), pp. 193–7. See also text to nn. 27–9 above.

33. See further Gill, *Personality*, 3.4.

34. This view is argued for strongly by G. Vlastos, *Socrates: Ironist and Moral Philosopher* (Cambridge, 1991), chs. 2–3. A similar view is taken, as regards Plato's *Apology*, by T. C. Brickhouse and N. D. Smith, *Socrates on Trial* (Princeton, 1989), and C. D. C. Reeve, *Socrates in the Apology* (Indianapolis, 1989). See also T. Penner, 'Socrates and the Early Dialogues', in R. Kraut, ed., *The Cambridge Companion in Plato* (Cambridge, 1992), pp. 121–69.

35. For a rare attempt to see in Aristophanes' *Clouds* a significant contribution to our evidence for the historical Socrates, see E. A. Havelock, 'The Socratic Self as it is Parodied in Aristophanes' *Clouds*', *Yale Classical Studies* 22 (1972), 1–18. On the history and fundamental difficulties of the Socratic problem, W. K. C. Guthrie, *A History of Greek Philosophy* (Cambridge, 1971) (=*HGP*) vol. 3, ch. 12, remains useful.

36. On one respect of the ancient reception of Socrates, see A. A. Long, 'Socrates in Hellenistic Philosophy', *CQ* NS 38 (1988), 150–71.

37. These considerations are among those that lead Brickhouse and Smith, *Socrates on Trial*, 3.3, esp. pp. 143–9, to regard the contradiction as less fundamental than it seems.

38. See further A. D. Woozley, 'Socrates on Disobeying the Law', in G. Vlastos, ed., *The Philosophy of Socrates* (Garden City, 1971), pp. 299–318; also Woozley, *Law and Obedience: The Arguments of Plato's* Crito (Chapel Hill, 1979). The question whether 'civil disobedience' is conceptually available in Greek culture forms part of this debate; another possible instance of this is Antigone's exemplary burial of her brother in defiance of Creon's edict, Sophocles, *Antigone*, esp. 450–70. On the related idea of an 'exemplary gesture', see text to n. 29 above.

39. See Pl. *Crito* 51b9–c1, also 'persuade or obey' in 51b3–4, 51e6–52a3. See R. Kraut, *Socrates and the State* (Princeton, 1984), ch. 3.

40. This is to raise the question of the function of the Platonic dialogue-form, and of whether this is to convey determinate doctrines or to present, and encourage, ongoing dialectical argument. On this issue, see e.g. C. L. Griswold, 'Plato's Metaphilosophy: Why Plato Wrote Dialogues', in C. L. Griswold, ed., *Platonic Writings, Platonic Readings* (London, 1988), pp. 143–67; M. Frede, 'Plato's Arguments and the Dialogue Form', in J. C. Klagge and N. D. Smith, *Methods of Interpreting Plato and his Dia-*

logues, *OSAP* supp. vol. (Oxford, 1992), pp. 201–19; C. Gill, 'Afterword: Dialectic and the Dialogue Form in Late Plato', in C. Gill and M. M. McCabe, edd., *Form and Argument in Late Plato* (Oxford, forthcoming). On the periods and chronology of Plato's writings, see Ch. V., n. 44.

41. The extent to which Socrates' 'divine' mission depends on Socrates' own reflective response to the divine messages received is stressed by Vlastos, *Socrates*, ch. 6, referring to e.g. *Apology* 21b, 28e.

42. Socrates is sometimes presented by Plato as perpetuating the heroic intensity of key poetic figures: see e.g. *Apology* 28c–d, alluding to Achilles' readiness to die, providing he can avenge Patroclus' death (*Il.* 18. 98–126).

43. This demand is implied in the Athenian Laws' concession that the citizen may persuade 'in accordance with the nature of justice', even if this fails to coincide with the Laws' normal command: see *Crito* 51b–c, and text to n. 39 above. Snell also stresses the combination of individual reasoning and an appeal to universal principles, but on a more Kantian picture of what properly moral reasoning requires; see *The Discovery of the Mind* (New York, 1960), pp. 182–90; see also Ch. III, text to nn. 5–6.

44. Socrates' 'paradoxes' are, principally, that virtue is one, that it is knowledge, and that nobody goes wrong willingly; for a full discussion of these, see G. X. Santas, *Socrates* (London, 1979). See further Vlastos, *Socrates*, pp. 3–5; examples of Socrates' claiming to have reached true conclusions are said to be *Gorgias* 473b, 479e. For the final versions of Vlastos's key articles on this question, see G. Vlastos, *Socratic Studies*, ed. M. Burnyeat (Cambridge, 1994), chs. 1–2.

45. C. Kahn, 'Drama and Dialectic in Plato's *Gorgias*', *OSAP* 1 (1983), 75–122. For a full-scale study of a Platonic dialogue that is broadly in line with Vlastos's approach, see W. T. Schmid, *On Manly Courage: A Study of Plato's* Laches (Carbondale, Illinois, 1992).

46. See e.g. R. Kraut, 'Comments on Vlastos' "The Socratic Elenchus"', *OSAP* 1 (1983), 59–70; J. Lesher, 'Socrates' Disavowal of Knowledge', *Journal of the History of Philosophy* 15 (1987), 275–88; and reviews of Vlastos, *Socrates*, by Kraut in *Philosophical Review* (1992), 353–8, and by C. D. C. Reeve in *Polis* 11 (1992), 72–82.

47. Pl. *Protagoras* 322d–326e; the term 'internalization' (for which, see Ch. III, text to n. 24) is mine, not Protagoras'; but it matches the process described, esp. in 325c–326e.

48. For this view, see e.g. T. Irwin, *Classical Thought* (Oxford, 1989), p. 61, referring to *Prt.* 325c–326e, taken with *Theaetetus* (*Tht.*) 167c, 172a–b; for doubts about this interpretation, see G. B. Kerferd, *The Sophistic Movement* (Cambridge, 1981), p. 130. On Protagorean relativism more generally, see e.g., Guthrie, *HGP*, vol. 3, pp. 170–5; Kerferd, *Sophistic Movement*, pp. 85–93. The difficulty of disentangling Protagoras' relativism from the Platonic elaboration of this is brought out, in connection with the *Theaetetus*, by M. Burnyeat, in *The* Theaetetus *of Plato*, tr. M. J. Levett, with introduction by Burnyeat (Indianapolis, 1990), pp. 7–19.

49. On Aristotle, see text to nn. 76–85 below. For surveys of Greek political theory, see E. Barker, *The Political Thought of Plato and Aristotle* (London, 1906, repr. 1959); T. A. Sinclair, *A History of Greek Political Thought* (London, 1951, 2nd edn. 1967); C. J. Rowe and M. Schofield, edd., *Cambridge History of Ancient Political Thought* (Cambridge, forthcoming).

50. This is true of Pl. *R.*, Aristotle, and the Stoics; see J. Annas, *The Morality of Happiness* (Oxford, 1993), chs. 15, 18–21, and (on the rather different position of the Epicureans), ch. 16. See further Ch. III, text to nn. 35, 45–58.

51. See text to nn. 46–8 above.

52. On this threefold division, see text to n. 11 above.

53. See K. R. Popper, *The Open Society and Its Enemies*, 2 vols. (London, 1945, 5th. edn, 1966); R. B. Levinson, *In Defense of Plato* (Cambridge, Mass., 1953); R. H. S. Crossman, *Plato Today* (London, 1963); J. R. Bambrough, ed., *Plato, Popper and Politics* (Cambridge, 1967).

54. See e.g. (in criticism of this way of analysing Plato) N. H. Dent, 'Moral Autonomy in the *Republic*', *Polis* 9 (1990), 52–77. For attempts to frame interpretative accounts which are closer to the ethical and political categories of the *Republic*, see e.g. Vlastos, 'The Theory of Social Justice in the *Polis* in Plato's *Republic*', in H. North, ed., *Interpretations of Plato*, Mnemosyne supp. vol. 50 (Leiden, 1977), pp. 1–40; Dent, 'Plato and Social Justice', in A. Loizou and H. Lesser, edd., Polis *and Politics: Essays in Greek Moral and Political Philosophy* (Aldershot, 1990), pp. 111–27.

55. On the special structure of the argument, see e.g. J. Annas, *An Introduction to Plato's* Republic (Oxford, 1981), esp. chs. 3–6; C. D. C. Reeve, *Philosopher-Kings: The Argument of Plato's* Republic (Princeton, 1988), esps. chs. 1, 3, 4; R. Kraut, 'The Defense of Justice in Plato's *Republic*', in Kraut, ed., *Cambridge Companion to Plato*, pp. 311–37.

56. For the ideas of the 'reason-ruled' *psuchē* and *polis*, see R. 441c–444e, taken with 427d–434d,

and 589c–592b. For two different approaches to the question of what 'reason' means in this connection, see T. Irwin, *Plato's Ethics* (Oxford, 1995), chs. 13, 15, 17, and Gill, *Personality*, ch. 4. On the (complex) meaning of 'reason' in Greek thought, see Ch. II, text to nn. 29–31.

57. Ch. III, text to nn. 67–71.

58. See esp. *R.* 490e–498c on the corruption of those with the 'philosophical nature' in the wrong kind of communal context, and 537d–539d, on the dangers of dialectic which is not based on the prior foundation of a sound character-development in the right kind of community. See also 413c–414b, 503a–e; also C. Gill, 'Plato and the Education of Character', *AGP* 67 (1985), 1–26.

59. See *R.* 498e–502e, esp. 498e and 500d–501b, taken with 400d–402c.

60. Thus e.g. Socrates makes it plain that he (who has not experienced the kind of education that he outlines) speaks with 'beliefs not knowledge' about the Form of the Good that is the goal of this programme, *R.* 506c–e, taken with 519b–521b. See C. Gill, 'Plato on Falsehood – not Fiction', in C. Gill and T. P. Wiseman, edd. *Lies and Fiction in the Ancient World* (Exeter, 1993), pp. 38–87, esp. p. 61, and Irwin, *Plato's Ethics*, p. 273. For possible exceptions to this general principle, see *R.* 496b–497a.

61. This point is acknowledged, by implication at least, in *R.* 498e–499d, 540d–541a, 592a–b, taken with refs. in nn. 58–60 above.

62. For different ways of bringing out this last point, see also J. Lear, 'In and Out of the *Republic*', *Phronesis* 38 (1992), 184–215; Reeve, *Philosopher-Kings*, esp, chs. 2, 5.

63. On Plato's thoughts on the role of women in the ideal state (*R.* 5), see Annas, *Introduction to Plato's* Republic, pp. 181–5, and refs. on her pp. 188–9; also S. M. Okin, *Women in Western Political Thought* (Princeton, 1979). On women in antiquity, the most recent survey is that of E. Fantham, H. P. Foley, N. B. Kampen, S. B. Pomeroy, and H. A. Shapiro, edd., *Women in the Classical World* (Oxford, 1995).

64. On the link between Greek and contemporary thinking about 'communities', see text to n. 7 above. However, Greek thinking about (e.g.) gender differs from (at least some versions of) 'gender-politics' or 'identity-politics', in that Greek thinkers see it as a requirement that they should place these aspects of human life in the larger context of the good life of the community, and do not merely argue for the claims of a particular group or perspective within the community.

65. See e.g. (embryos) *Laws* 775, 788–90; (the symposium) 637–50; (religious rituals) 772; (women as helping to shape ethical attitudes) 781, 784a–c, 808a. On *Laws* in general, see T. J. Saunders's Penguin Classics tr. with introduction (Harmondsworth, 1970); also his *Plato's Penal Code: Tradition, Controversy, and Reform in Greek Penology* (Oxford, 1991), part 2; R. F. Stalley, *An Introduction to Plato's* Laws (Oxford, 1983); G. Morrow, *Plato's Cretan City: A Historical Interpretation of the* Laws (Princeton, 1960); see further text to n. 74.

66. See *Laws* 739 and contrast *R.* 462–6; also, on the direction of the community with a view to the realization of virtue, see e.g. *Laws* 643a–644b, 716–17, 732e–734e, 964c–965a. For refs. on the relationship between *R.* and *Laws*, see n. 74 below.

67. On earlier (as well as later) Greek political theory, see D. Kagan, *The Great Dialogue: History of Greek Political Thought from Homer in Polybius* (New York, 1965).

68. See text to nn. 54–6 above; hence, it is notoriously difficult to form any precise view about the ethical and political status of the third class in the ideal state; see e.g. B. Williams's (critical) treatment of the theory in 'The Analogy of City and Soul in Plato's *Republic*', in E. N. Lee, A. P. D. Mourelatos, and R. M. Rorty, edd., *Exegesis and Argument* (Assen, 1973), pp. 196–206.

69. See *Statesman* 291d–311c, esp. 293c–e, 297b–c, 300a–d, 309a–d, 310e–311c. See further C. J. Rowe, ed., *Reading the* Statesman: *Proceedings of the III Symposium Platonicum* (St. Augustin, 1995), which contains both M. Lane, 'A New Angle on Utopia: The Political Theory of the *Statesman*', pp. 276–91, and C. Gill, 'Rethinking Constitutionalism in *Statesman* 291–303', pp. 292–305; see also Rowe, '*Politicus*: Structure and Form', in Gill and McCabe, edd., *Form and Argument in Late Plato* (Oxford, forthcoming). For the view that the *Statesman* is 'constitutionalist' in a stronger sense than this, see e.g. G. Klosko, *The Development of Plato's Political Theory* (New York, 1986), p. 194.

70. See *Laws* 735–68, 960–8. Like the ideal Athens of the Atlantis story in Plato's *Timaeus* 21–6, *Critias* 109–12, this can be taken as an ideal version of the Solonian, pre-Persian Wars, 'moderate' democracy; on the political implications of the Atlantis story, see C. Gill, 'The Genre of the Atlantis Story', *Classical Philology* 72 (1977), 287–304, esp. pp. 294–8; and P. Vidal-Naquet, 'Athènes et Atlantis', *Revue des Études Greques* 77 (1964), 420–44.

71. See text to nn. 65–6 above and nn. 74–5 below.

72. See text to nn. 57–62 above, and on the normative sense of 'reason', Ch. II, text to nn. 29–31.

73. See refs. in n. 69 above; also C. L. Griswold, '*Politikē Epistēmē* in Plato's *Statesman*', in J. P. Anton and A. Preus, edd., *Essays in Ancient Greek Philosophy*, vol. 3 (Albany, NY, 1989), pp. 141–67.

74. See e.g. 718–23, 809–12, 890, 899d–900b, 964b–965a. See A. Laks, 'Legislation and Demiurgy: on the Relationship between Plato's *Republic* and *Laws*', *Classical Antiquity* 9 (1990), 209–29; C. Bobonich, 'Persuasion, Compulsion and Freedom in Plato's *Laws*', *CQ* NS 41 (1991), 365–88, and 'Reading the *Laws*', in Gill and McCabe, edd., *Form and Argument in Late Plato* (forthcoming). See further, on the place of the *Laws* in Plato's political thinking, T. J. Saunders, 'Plato's Later Political Thought', in Kraut, ed., *Cambridge Companion to Plato*, pp. 464–92.

75. See Ch. III, text to nn. 22–5.

76. *NE* 1. 7, esp. 1097b11, *Pol.* 1. 2, esp. 1252b29–1253a5. See further W. Kullmann, 'Man as Political Animal in Aristotle', in D. Keyt and F. Miller, edd., *A Companion to Aristotle's* Politics (Oxford, 1991) (hereafter Keyt and Miller), pp. 94–117.

77. Hence, Aristotle dismisses the concept of the 'minimalist state' (as a mere 'guarantee of just claims') proposed by Lycophron, *Pol.* 3. 9, esp. 1280b8–12. For related reasons, he has reservations about democracy, as a constitution which presents freedom (understood as 'living as one pleases') as the greatest good; see e.g. 5. 9, esp. 1310a28–38, 6. 2, esp. 1317b11. See also *Pol.* 3. 4, 7. 1–3 on the linkage between human happiness and the community.

78. Aristotle is sometimes thought to see the individual simply as part of an 'organic' state, e.g. because of *Pol.* 1. 2, 1253a18–23 (i.e. he is thought to hold a 'totalitarian' view of the relationship between the state and the individual; see e.g. Popper, *The Open Society and its Enemies*, vol. 2, pp. 1–26). This interpretation of his view rests on a distinction which is, arguably, alien to Greek thought; see section 1 above.

79. The issue of *NE* 10. 7–8 (on which, see Ch. III, text to nn. 72–81) whether practical or theoretical wisdom constitutes the best possible form of human happiness is referred to in *Pol.* 7. 2, esp. 1324a23–1324b2; see further D. J. Depew, 'Politics, Music and Contemplation in Aristotle's Ideal State', in Keyt and Miller, pp. 346–80. But the capacity for rule is not defined by Aristotle by reference to dialectically-based knowledge.

80. See further C. J. Rowe, 'Aims and Methods in Aristotle's *Politics*', in Keyt and Miller, pp. 57–74; Irwin, *Aristotle's First Principles*, pp. 352–5, 466–8; also, more generally, R. G. Mulgan, *Aristotle's Political Theory* (Oxford, 1977).

81. See *Pol.* 3. 9–13. See further M. von Leyden, *Aristotle on Equality and Justice: His Political Argument* (London, 1985); F. D. Miller, 'Aristotle on Natural Law and Justice', in Keyt and Miller, pp. 279–306; M. C. Nussbaum, 'Nature, Function and Capability: Aristotle on Political Distribution', in Patzig, ed., *Aristotles Politik*, pp. 153–76.

82. See text to n. 70 above; on the 'mixed' constitution preferred by both these works, the standard work is still K. von Fritz, *The Theory of the Mixed Constitution in Antiquity* (New York, 1954).

83. See *Pol.* 7–8, esp. 7. 1–3, 17; 8. 1, 5; Pl. *Laws* is discussed by Aristotle in 2. 6.

84. See e.g. Irwin, *Aristotle's First Principles*, pp. 416–23.

85. See *Pol.* 1. 4–6, 12–13; on this aspect of Pl. *R.*, see text to n. 63 above. See e.g. W. W. Fortenbaugh, 'Aristotle on Slaves and Women', in J. Barnes, M. Schofield, and R. Sorabji, edd., *Articles on Aristotle*, vol. 2: *Ethics and Politics* (London, 1977), pp. 135–9; M. Schofield, 'Ideology and Philosophy in Aristotle's Theory of Slavery, in Patzig, ed., *Aristoteles Politik*, pp. 1–27; also, more generally, F. D. Miller, *Nature, Justice, and Rights in Aristotle's* Politics (Oxford, 1995). On Aristotle's teleological approach, see Ch. V, text to nn. 8–11, 60–72.

86. Three revised translations of Arist. *Pol.* with introductions and notes have appeared recently: with introduction by S. Everson for the Cambridge Texts in the History of Political Thought (Cambridge, 1988); by T. J. Saunders for Penguin Classics (Harmondsworth, 1981); by R. F. Stalley for The World's Classics (Oxford, 1995). See also T. J. Saunders's own translation of Plato, *Laws* (Harmondsworth, 1970); also C. J. Rowe, *Plato*: Statesman (text, translation and Introduction) (Warminster, 1995); Plato: *Statesman*, tr. with introduction and notes by J. Annas and R. Waterfield for the Cambridge Texts in the History of Political Thought (Cambridge, 1995).

87. A. A. Long and D. N. Sedley, *The Hellenistic Philosophers* (Cambridge, 1987) (=LS), vol. 1, translations and commentary, vol. 2, texts, notes and bibliography, is a contribution of fundamental importance; on Epicurean and Stoic social and political thinking, see sections 22 and 67. See also A. Laks and M. Schofield, edd., *Justice and Generosity: Studies in Hellenistic Social and Political Philosophy* (Cambridge, 1995).

88. See LS 67A–E (also F–G, on Chrysippus); on Plato, see n. 63 above. This represents the more

Cynic side of Stoicism; on Cynicism and Stoicism, see J. Rist, *Stoic Philosophy* (Cambridge, 1969), ch. 4. On Cynicism, D. R. Dudley, *A History of Cynicism* (London, 1937), remains useful; see also A. J. Malherbe, ed., *The Cynic Epistles: A Study Edition* (Missoula, Montana, 1977).

89. See esp. LS 67A(1), B(4); see further M. Schofield, *The Stoic Idea of the City* (Cambridge, 1991), chs. 1–2, and J. Annas's review of Schofield in *Polis* 11 (1992), 95–101. See also A. Erskine, *The Hellenistic Stoa: Political Thought and Action* (London, 1990).

90. On the Stoic understanding of what 'nature' means, see Ch. V, text to nn. 74–85.

91. On 'appropriate actions' or 'proper functions' in Stoic ethics, see LS 59; see further I. G. Kidd, 'Stoic Intermediates and the End for Man', in A. A. Long, ed., *Problems in Stoicism* (London, 1971), pp. 150–72.

92. See Cicero *De Officiis* (*On Duties*), 1–2, esp. 1. 107–21; for a good tr., see that of M. T. Griffin and E. M. Atkins (Cambridge Texts in the History of Political Thought, Cambridge, 1991). See further P. H. De Lacy, 'The Four Stoic *Personae*', *Illinois Classical Studies* 2 (1977), 163–72; A. A. Long, 'Greek Ethics After MacIntyre and the Stoic Community of Reason', *Ancient Philosophy* 3 (1983), 174–99; C. Gill, 'Personhood and Personality: the Four-*Personae* Theory in Cicero, *De Officiis* 1', *OSAP* 6 (1988), 169–99. For a similar point, made about a wider range of Hellenistic and Roman writings, see C. Gill, 'Peace of Mind and Being Yourself: Panaetius to Plutarch', in W. Haase and H. Temporini, edd., *Aufstieg und Niedergang der römischen Welt* II.36.7 (Berlin, 1994), pp. 4599–4640. For refs. on more radical types of modern individualism, see n. 2 above.

93. See LS K–L, R–S; also Schofield, *Stoic Idea of the City*, chs. 3–4; G. Striker, 'The Origins of Natural Law', *Proceedings of the Boston Area Colloquium in Ancient Philosophy* 2 (1986), 79–94.

94. See LS 67 A(1), B(3), also 57 F(= Cicero, *De Finibus* 3. 62–8), and 57 G. For Cicero's fusion of this idea with more conventional patterns of relationship, see *De Officiis* 1. 50–60. See further Annas, *Morality of Happiness*, pp. 262–76. On the question how far the Stoic validation of generalized other-benefiting motivation constitutes a change from the typical Greek validation of mutual benefit, rather than altruism (on the view suggested in Ch. III above), see C. Gill, 'Altruism or Reciprocity in Greek Ethical Philosophy?', in C. Gill, N. Postlethwaite, and R. Seaford, edd., *Reciprocity in Ancient Greece* (Oxford, forthcoming).

95. See LS 22 A–B, M; for related reasons, Epicurus stresses that justice of this type takes different forms in different societies, according to the needs of each society, and that, in conventional societies, fear of punishment is needed to induce people to obey laws. See LS. vol. 1, pp. 134–7, linking this theory with 5–4th c. ideas about justice as a 'social contract'; also A. A. Long, 'Pleasure and Social Utility – the Virtues of Being Epicurean', in H. Flashar and O. Gigon, edd., *Aspect de la philosophie hellénistique*, Fondation Hardt, *Entretiens sur l'antiquité classique*, vol. 32 (Vandoeuvres-Geneva, 1986), pp. 283–324; Annas, *Morality of Happiness*, pp. 293–302.

96. The stages of human civilization are (1) pre-linguistic and pre-social; (2) pre-linguistic family and neighbourhood alliances; (3) social and political structures formed to counteract the mutual violence motivated by false beliefs about what is valuable. See Lucretius, *De Rerum Natura* 5, esp. 925–38, 953–61, 1011–27, 1105–57 (=LS 22 J–L). See also J. Nichols, *Epicurean Political Philosophy: The De Rerum Natura of Lucretius* (Ithaca, 1976), ch. 4; C. P. Segal, *Lucretius on Death and Anxiety: Poetry and Philosophy in De Rerum Natura* (Princeton, 1990), ch. 5; and M. C. Nussbaum, *The Therapy of Desire* (Princeton, 1994), ch. 7.

97. See LS 22 S, and M (3–4); also LS, vol. 1, p. 136.

98. See Cic. *Fin.* 1. 47, taken with LS 21 A–B, esp. B (6), H–I; see further P. Mitsis, *Epicurus' Ethical Theory* (Ithaca, 1988), ch. 2, esp. pp. 74–6.

99. See Ch. III, text to nn. 56–8.

100. This is clearer in the case of the Epicureans than the Stoics (on the relevant strand of Stoicism, see text to nn. 88–90 above); it can be linked with such features as their 'worship' of Epicurus as a quasi-god and the strongly 'missionary' character of the school. See further B. Frischer, *The Sculpted Word: Epicureanism and Philosophical Recruitment in Ancient Greece* (Berkeley, 1982); Nussbaum, *Therapy of Desire*, ch. 4.

V. THE NORMS OF NATURE[1]

1. *The Issue: Nature and Ethics*

In this chapter, I take up a question which follows from the issues discussed in the previous ones. I have considered ways in which Greek thought, both as expressed in poetry and philosophy, assumes that there are objective norms, in psychology, ethics, and politics.[2] This gives rise to the question: what is the ultimate basis for these norms? I focus on one kind of answer to this question, and on the debate from which this answer arises. This answer is that the normative basis for psychological, ethical, and political life exists in 'nature', in some sense. Versions of this answer can be found in, for instance, Plato, Aristotle, the Stoics and Epicureans; and their answers build on fifth-century controversy about the relationship between ethics and nature, as well as developing an important feature of Presocratic thinking.

This topic has given rise to an interesting recent debate (one that relates to those discussed earlier in this book) about the role of 'nature' in Greek ethical thought and about the relationship between Greek and modern thinking in this respect. This debate needs to be set in the larger context of the history of Western thought on this question. In the Medieval period, and, to a lesser extent, in the Renaissance and subsequently, morality was seen as underpinned by Christianity, which was associated with a particular conception of the universe. The advance of science from the Renaissance onwards was, typically, seen as threatening this conception, together with the associated religious and moral ideals.[3] In the Enlightenment, claims for the 'naturalness' of morality tended to be stated in secular terms. For instance, Kant claimed that the capacity for the moral response, as he understood this (namely as the capacity for 'autonomy', exercised in legislating universal laws for oneself) was a fundamental (or 'transcendental') capacity of human beings as such.[4] In the early twentieth century, a well-known position, stated memorably in G. E. Moore's *Principia Ethica* (Cambridge, 1903), was that questions about nature and about morality belonged to fundamentally different categories of enquiry. Any kind of 'ethical naturalism' was misguided, and involved the 'naturalistic fallacy', that of making an illegitimate move from an 'is' to an 'ought'. However, not all subsequent philosophers have agreed with this view. There have been a number of modern attempts to construct theories designed to prove to *anyone* (regardless of her moral character or beliefs) that it is rational to be morally good. Such attempts have centred on hypothetical models such as the 'prisoner's dilemma' or 'the veil of ignorance' (alleged to show that justice is the best policy), or on the claim that a true understanding of human rationality or of personal identity leads to the conclusion that everyone has reason to be morally good.[5] These modern theories may be seen as contemporary versions of the idea that moral norms are grounded in what is, in some sense, 'natural' for human beings.

Alasdair MacIntyre and Bernard Williams are, for partly different reasons, highly sceptical of the validity of the modern attempts to claim that morality is natural, both as regards the Kantian version of this claim and the more recent versions of John Rawls and others.[6] Williams is also sceptical about Plato's apparent attempt to prove to *anyone* (even the immoralist, Thrasymachus) that justice constitutes happiness.[7] However, both thinkers believe that Aristotle's version of this claim (especially in his presentation of the virtuous life as the 'human function' in *NE* 1. 7) represents a more credible version of the appeal to nature. MacIntyre emphasizes the idea that, for this appeal to be credible, the idea of human nature employed must reflect the ideals already current in the thinker's community.[8] Williams stresses rather the thought that the kind of moral attitudes allegedly grounded in human nature must match those which are already part of the ethical agent's character and beliefs.[9] Although both thinkers regard Aristotle's use of this idea as philosophically credible in its own time, they also think that this kind of claim is no longer conceptually possible for us, for two principal reasons. (1) They think that Aristotle's move presupposes a degree of consistency between scientific and moral perspectives which is no longer open to us. For Aristotle, as they interpret him, either there is complete consistency between these two (separate) perspectives, or these perspectives form parts of a single world-view.[10] (2) They think that the world-view thus constructed is unified or 'harmonious' in a way that we cannot now accept. These views are reflected in these two comments, by Williams and MacIntyre respectively:

Aristotle saw a certain kind of ethical, cultural, and indeed political life as a harmonious culmination of human potentialities, recoverable from an absolute understanding of nature. We have no reason to believe in that.

Aristotle has no moral conception of human life which is not already in its own way a scientific and a metaphysical conception and no scientific or metaphysical conception which is not already in its own way a moral conception.[11]

Some recent scholarly discussions have argued that the interpretations by Williams and MacIntyre of Aristotle's use of the idea of human nature in *NE* 1. 7 need to be qualified in certain ways, and that this has a bearing on the question of the relationship between Greek and modern thinking on this topic. Two main points have been made. One is that the Greek appeal to the idea of 'nature' as a norm is a move that is made, by Aristotle and the Stoics at least, *within* ethical theory. It is not an attempt to support ethics 'from outside', by appealing to a (separately conceived) scientific account. Williams and MacIntyre accept that Aristotle at least is not trying to prove *to anyone* that his ethical ideas can be supported 'scientifically'. But some scholars would stress even more than they do that, for several Greek thinkers, a proper grasp of the ethical significance of nature depends on a combination of the development of ethical character with understanding of the natural world.[12] Second, it has been argued that Greek thinkers do not believe that the kind of ethical-*cum*-scientific world-view provided in this way is, necessarily, unified or harmonious in the way that Williams suggests. The resulting outlook may contain certain kinds of inherent tension of conflict (for instance, between the claims of practical and contemplative wisdom) as well as being in conflict with conventional Greek ethical attitudes.[13] More generally, Julia Annas, in *The Morality of Happiness*, argues that Greek thinking of this type is very different from what is understood as 'ethical naturalism' in modern philosophy; and that we need to recognize this if we are to make sense of the (relatively complex) way in which the idea of nature is used in Aristotle and Hellenistic philosophy.[14]

In this chapter, I consider the history of Greek thinking about the idea of nature as a moral norm against the background of this recent intellectual and scholarly debate. As well as considering this question in connection with Aristotle and Hellenistic philosophy, I look at the preceding history of this theme in Greek philosophy. How far, for instance, can we find in earlier Greek thinkers the relatively sophisticated approach to this question that Annas, for instance, ascribes to Aristotle and the Stoics? An obvious difficulty in doing so is that the separation of distinct branches of philosophy (such as ethics, physics, and logic) is not a feature of Greek philosophy before Aristotle. The Presocratics, in particular, frame their theories in a way that involves a very close connection between normative ideals and innovative ideas about nature. It is not appropriate, then, to say that the idea of nature functions for them as a norm *within* ethical theory. However, in their case too, we can sometimes ask to what extent they think that a proper understanding of nature depends on, or goes hand in hand with, ethical or psychological development. I suggest that this is one of the most well-marked features of Greek thinking from the Presocratics to Hellenistic philosophy. In this respect, Greek thinkers of all periods avoid making the move criticized by Williams and MacIntyre, of trying to prove to *anyone*, regardless of his ethical character, that it is rational to be morally good.[15] Although the larger question of the relationship between Greek and modern thinking on this topic falls outside the scope of this book, I do want to suggest that, on this point, Greek thinking emerges as more credible to modern readers than might have been expected.

There is one further general consideration that bears on this question, relating to Greek religion and ethics. For modern Western scholars, it is easy to approach this topic with misleading parallels with Christianity in mind. As noted earlier, in Western culture since antiquity, morality has been seen as grounded in a Christian world-view, and science has often been seen as threatening this world-view and the morality that is associated with this. The relationship between religion, ethics, and science in Greek culture is very different and in some ways more complex. The ethically problematic status of the Greek gods was underlined in central genres of Greek poetry from the *Iliad* onwards, especially in Attic tragedy.[16] A recurrent strand in Greek thought was concerned either to reject the (ethically problematic) religion of the poetic tradition, or to reconceive 'god' and 'the divine' in a more ethically acceptable form.[17] In the absence of an orthodox religious conception of the universe, Greek thinkers were relatively free to offer their own accounts of the natural world, with very varying degrees and kinds of role allocated to 'the divine'.[18] In so far as the account of the natural world was taken to have ethical significance, this significance might or might not be linked with the role of the divine (or with human aspirations toward the divine). In other words, the question of the relationship between 'god', 'nature', and ethical norms (however these norms were defined) was itself one that formed a central part of debate, rather than being a matter of accepting (or questioning) a received religious and moral world view.[19]

2. *Presocratics and Fifth-Century Debate*

The evidence for Presocratic philosophy raises a number of difficulties for anyone pursuing this question, one of which (the absence of a clear distinction between branches of thought) has already been noted.[20] None the less, I think that it is possible to identify a certain line of thought on this question in our evidence for, for instance, Heraclitus, Empedocles, and

Pythagoras, as interpreted in some recent work.[21] These thinkers do not only see normative ideas (such as 'reason', 'friendship' and 'harmony') as applying equally to nature (as they understand this) and human psychology and social behaviour. They also suggest, in different ways, that the understanding of the truth of their account of nature (and hence the recognition of its normative content) is linked with, and depends on, a certain kind of psychological or ethical progress by the person gaining this understanding.

For instance, the *logos* ('reason') for Heraclitus is an idea which functions at several levels. It is at once the principle of cosmic order, the rationality underlying apparent contradiction and change, and the core of the philosophical message (the rational discourse) that Heraclitus seeks to convey. In another sense, it is the 'one wise' which (on a correct interpretation of what 'Zeus' means) 'is willing to be called by the name of Zeus'. To gain a proper understanding of the *logos*, what is needed is not just intellectual concentration but the kind of shaping of one's life and character that reproduces in oneself the underlying order of the *kosmos*.[22] M. R. Wright puts the point in these terms:[23]

The possession of 'dry' soul – that which is 'wisest and best' – is a state achieved by a continuing victory over impulse, reinforced by intellectual dedication; in this state of 'super-awakeness', awareness of the unseen *harmonia* governing the functioning of the cosmos becomes possible. The self-increasing *logos* of the soul makes contact with the 'one wise' which steers all things, and this in turn enlarges the soul's potential for wisdom.

Heraclitus' famously provocative and riddling style also conveys the idea that the proper understanding of his account of nature, and of the norm that this embodies (the *logos*), requires his listeners to 'search themselves' as well as the principles of nature to find the hidden truth.[24]

A broadly similar pattern of ideas can be seen to Empedocles, who wrote two poems (*On Nature* and *Purifications*), which some scholars see as closely linked in their thought.[25] *On Nature* interprets nature in terms of the competing operation of two fundamental principles, love and strife, on the four basic elements (earth, air, fire, and water). Thought is conceived as the highest possible synthesis of these elements; at its best, it is identified with god, or the 'holy mind', and with the perfect, spherical shape.[26] In *Purifications*, similar ideas are presented in religious and moral terms. Empedocles presents himself as having passed through a stage of strife (associated with dispersal into separate elements) to a 'purification' which brings about the 'divine' synthesis of these elements through the operation of love.[27] In *Purifications*, he urges his fellow-citizens to achieve a similar state by mutual cooperativeness; in *On Nature*, he urges the addressee,

Pausanias, to do so by a combination of intellectual effort and 'good will in pure exercises'.[28] As in Heraclitus, the understanding of the nature of the universe and of its ethical significance depends on a special kind of ethical and cognitive process, the final outcome of which is the equivalent on the human level of the best possible ('divine') state of the natural order.

For these and most other Presocratics, the main outcome of their enquiry for the larger community was the attempt by the thinkers to communicate the core of their ideas, and to urge others to seek to understand these truths (which are, typically, obscure or unconventional in thought) for themselves.[29] Pythagoras, however, seems to have formed a community based on his teachings, as well as exercising political dominance in Croton in the late sixth century. In Pythagorean thought, the idea of 'harmony' serves both as the central cosmic principle (one that could be analysed further in terms of a complex number-theory) and as an ethical norm, setting the pattern for diet, daily life, and social relationships. Although the problems raised by the nature of the evidence are especially acute in this case,[30] we can find here too indications of the idea that a proper understanding of the true 'harmony' of nature is linked with realizing this in your own life and character, and thus achieving the kind of 'divinity' that constitutes the best possible natural state.[31]

What we do not, I think, find in our evidence for the Presocratics are indications that they discussed, in any systematic way, the philosophical implications of connecting ethical norms and the study of nature in this way.[32] But the question of the relationship between *phusis* ('nature') and *nomos* ('law', 'convention', or 'ethics') certainly did play a central part in the debates among intellectuals, including Socrates and the sophists, in the latter half of the fifth century and the early fourth century at Athens.[33] However, in spite of the fact that natural philosophers, such as Anaxagoras, were active at this time and stimulated some of this debate, there is no clear indication that the line of thought discussed here (text to nn. 21–31 above) was explicitly considered in the course of this debate.

The principal positions in this debate, as usually defined by scholars, are these.[34] Some thinkers (such as Antiphon and the figure of Callicles in Plato's *Gorgias*) argue that there is a fundamental gap between natural human desires and the legal or moral constraints of communal life.[35] A variant of this position is that there is a 'law of nature' that legitimates the ruthless pursuit of advantage by states, even if this runs counter to the normal rules of conduct governing relations between states.[36] A divergent view is that human nature is such that we can only survive and lead tolerable lives by framing legal rules and by developing ethical attitudes. This (broadly) 'Utilitarian' position is adopted by Plato's Protagoras, as outlined earlier.[37] A related view is that laws and ethics constitute a 'social contract' (usually conceived as implied rather than explicit), the aim of which is to avoid the mutual violence that human nature would generate without such a contract.[38] This is a significantly weaker position than that found in several later Greek thinkers, including Plato, Aristotle, and the Stoics, according to which human beings are naturally adapted to live virtuous lives and to form communities which are the proper context of such lives.[39]

This debate about law and nature seems to have been stimulated by a variety of factors, including increasing contact between Greek and non-Greek cultures (promoting a relativistic view of ethical norms) and the pressure on Greek political and communal structures caused by the prolonged Peloponnesian War.[40] What seems clear is that natural philosophy, especially that occurring within this period (such as that of Anaxagoras and Diogenes of Apollonia)[41] tended to be interpreted in the light of this debate, regardless of whether or not this was an appropriate framework for understanding such philosophy. It is clear from, for instance, Aristophanes' *Clouds*, Plato's *Apology* and (much later) his *Laws*, that any kind of 'naturalist' speculation could be seen as outright rejection of the traditional world-view (including gods) rather than as the reconceiving of nature and the role of the divine.[42] It is also clear that this kind of speculation about nature could also be taken as implying the rejection of conventional ethics; that is, the kind of position linked above with Antiphon or Callicles. Socrates, as presented by Plato in the early dialogues, conspicuously abstains from this type of natural theorizing.[43] Nor is he presented in Plato's early dialogues as questioning natural philosophers (for instance, Anaxagoras) about the implications of their thought for the relationship between ethics and nature. For reasons of this kind, we do not find in our evidence for the late fifth and early fourth century a sympathetic response to, or a searching examination of, the type of Presocratic thinking outlined earlier (text to nn. 21–31).

3. *Plato and Aristotle*

However, from the works of Plato's middle period onwards,[44] we do find the continuation and examination of the line of thought discussed in the Presocratics, particularly in Plato and the Stoics. In Plato's *Phaedo* and *Timaeus*, for instance, we find two, partly contrasted, responses. In both dialogues, Plato's main speakers indicate their support for what might be called a 'providential' view of nature: that is, one that shows that the natural world constitutes an ordered system shaped 'for the best'. In the *Phaedo*, this view leads Socrates to reject Anaxagoras' account of the natural world, because (despite giving a key role to 'mind', *nous*), the account is not providential in character.[45] In the *Timaeus*, on the other hand, Timaeus offers an extended account of the natural world as an ordered and providentially conceived whole. Although Plato has, clearly, drawn on a number of earlier theories, the Pythagorean idea of the natural world as a 'harmony' that lends itself to detailed mathematical analysis is an important source of inspiration.[46]

In both dialogues, we also find the idea that the development of knowledge of the truth contributes to, or depends on, the development of virtuous attitudes and patterns of emotion and desire. In the *Phaedo*, the relevant idea is that knowledge of the truth (conceived as knowledge of the Forms) depends on, and promotes, the kind of purification of reason from body-based emotions and desires that is necessary for real virtue (courage, self-control, and so forth).[47] In the *Timaeus*, in line with the view of nature as providentially ordered, human beings are conceived as (essentially) complex psychophysical wholes. Accordingly, emphasis is placed on the idea that humans can be disabled from gaining virtue by the wrong type of physiological make-up, and also that a proper education and way of life should help to match bodily and psychological functions to each other.[48] But here too, we find the idea that knowledge (now rather differently conceived) can contribute towards the ordering of one's own psycho-ethical state: that one can become more *kosmios* ('ordered') by correct understanding of the *kosmos*, and that this can help to correct any 'disharmony' in one's character. Although this is presented as a proper goal for any human being, it is also made clear that knowledge will only have this 'ordering' effect in the case of someone who already has a relatively developed combination of philosophical understanding and a virtuously 'harmonized' character.[49]

The *Republic* contains, as we have seen already, a complex two-stage account of full ethical education, consisting, first, of the pre-dialectical development of ethical character and, then, of the kind of post-dialectical knowledge that shapes character further.[50] The account of the second, intellectual, stage of education does not explicitly include study of the natural world or of human nature. It is made up of a combination of mathematical and dialectical studies, though it includes a rigorously mathematical version of astronomy.[51] The way in which (and the extent to which) this two-stage programme is designed to produce ethical motivation is a topic of much recent debate. Terence Irwin, for instance, in two major studies, interprets Plato's account in terms of the idea that the proper understanding of oneself as a rational agent generates the motivation to benefit others.[52] However, it is possible to interpret the programme in a way which is closer to the approach of the Presocratic thinkers discussed earlier and to that of the *Timaeus*. We may take it that the 'harmonization' of the *psuchē* produced by the first phase of education (which is a prerequisite for the second stage) is amenable to rational analysis in mathematical or quasi-mathematical terms. Philosophers who have completed both stages of the programme are capable of carrying out this kind of analysis, and hence both of consolidating the 'order' in their own characters and of designing the communal patterns that will help to produce prereflective 'harmony' in the characters of others.[53]

These scholars who have explored this line of interpretation most fully are those, especially H.-J. Krämer, who believe that Plato's most profound type of philosophizing was the highly abstract and systematic type of theory (Plato's so-called 'unwritten doctrines') for which we have considerable evidence from Aristotle and other later writers in antiquity.[54] This approach to Plato is highly influential in Germany and Italy, though British and American scholars have mostly been much more sceptical about its validity.[55] However, M. F. Burnyeat, a leading British scholar of ancient philosophy, thinks that our reports of the 'unwritten doctrines' may reflect Plato's work in the Academy at the time of the composition of the *Republic*.[56] Whether or not we make reference to the 'unwritten doctrines', the line of thought outlined in the previous paragraph is compatible, at least, with the Pythagorean-style analysis of the 'order' of nature (including that of the *psuchē*) that we find in the *Timaeus*.[57] The feature of Plato's thinking, as so interpreted, that interests me most is this. Plato does not suppose that an understanding of the natural order will be able, by itself, to persuade *anyone* that they should be virtuous. It is only those who have already developed virtuous characters, at the pre-reflective level, who are capable of understanding properly the significance of the natural order that is the object of philosophical understanding. It is the *combination* of the pre-reflective virtue (the 'harmony' in the *psuchē*) and post-reflective understanding of nature that enables one to grasp this significance and also to become specially 'ordered' in one's own character.[58] As we shall see, a rather similar idea can be found in some later thinkers too; the Presocratics discussed earlier stress rather the idea that post-reflective understanding goes hand in hand with (or brings with it) development in ethical character.[59]

With Aristotle, we return to the question with which this chapter opened, that of the status of the idea of 'nature' (especially 'human nature') in ethics. In Aristotle, this question arises in a more clearly defined way because he is the first Greek philosopher to distinguish ethics, as a branch of philosophy, from, for instance, physics, metaphysics, and psychology.[60] This gives rise to the question how closely the ideas of ethics are integrated with those of these other branches of enquiry, a question on which scholars take very different positions. Martha Nussbaum, for instance, argues that, for Aristotle, ethics is characterized by the adoption of a distinctively practical and 'human' perspective on the nature of happiness, by contrast with Plato's aspiration towards a 'divine' or cosmic perspective in the *Republic* and elsewhere.[61] Jonathan Lear, by contrast, thinks that, for Aristotle, the pursuit of human happiness in ethical philosophy must take into account the fact (which is reflected also in Aristotle's metaphysical and psychological works) that human beings, as a species, are constitutively capable of aspiring towards a 'god-like' understanding of the truth about nature.[62]

The key texts on this question are Aristotle's characterization of happiness by reference to the idea of a 'human function' in *NE* 1. 7 and the contrast between 'human' and 'divine' forms of virtue in *NE* 10. 7–8.[63] These texts raise two overlapping issues: that of the extent to which they appeal to a conception of what is 'natural' that depends on non-ethical thought, and that of the consistency between these two important passages in the *Nicomachean Ethics*. On l. 7, as noted earlier, thinkers such as MacIntyre and Williams assume that Aristotle is appealing to a conception of human nature which is based on a broader enquiry than that of ethics (which MacIntyre calls 'metaphysical biology').[64] However, other scholars, including Annas, have argued that Aristotle is using the idea of the 'human function' as a normative idea *within* ethical enquiry. On the latter interpretation, when Aristotle defines his account of happiness in terms of the 'human function', he is appealing to the *ethical agent's* understanding of what it is to be essentially human: that is, to centre one's life on 'an activity of the *psuchē* according to virtue' (1098a16–17).[65] However, neither MacIntyre nor Williams nor these other scholars think that Aristotle is using the idea of the 'human function' as an 'Archimedean' point, to persuade *anyone* that the facts of human nature mean that they have a reason to be ethically good.[66] In general, Aristotle lays down as a prerequisite for worthwhile ethical enquiry that one should have a grasp of 'the facts' of ethical life (pre-reflective virtue in one's habits and attitudes) before going on to examine the 'reason' for this;[67] and he can be taken as assuming that grasp here. One can adopt this interpretation of Aristotle without denying that this account of human nature, as far as it goes, *is* consistent with the picture of distinctively human capacities that is provided by other branches of enquiry;[68] but Aristotle's argument in *NE* 1. 7 does not *depend* on non-ethical enquiries.

On *NE* 10. 7–8, I have already stated my preference for the view that the later discussion can be seen as consistent with *NE* 1. 7,[69] and with the positive valuation of ethical virtue in much of *NE*. Aristotle can be seen as presuming in 10. 7–8 an audience that already sees the combination of ethical virtue and practical wisdom as our distinctively 'human' function. But he seeks also to persuade this audience that our capacity for philosophically-based knowledge is our 'divine' one, and that we should direct our lives in the light of this (complex) truth.[70] In putting forward this view, he may, as Lear argues, be presuming the conception of what 'god' means in the *Metaphysics*, in addition to the distinction between practical wisdom (*phronēsis*) and contemplative or philosophical wisdom (*sophia*) drawn in *NE* 6.[71] But it can be argued that his account in *NE* 10. 7–8 does not depend on specific, technical claims made in non-ethical works. What Aristotle presumes is an audience which both (1) recognizes the idea that our 'human' function is fulfilled through the exercise of ethical virtue and (2) can be led, by their experience of philosophy, to accept the idea that the achievement of philosophical knowledge constitutes our 'divine' function.[72] As in the case of *NE* 1. 7, Aristotle, presumably, thinks that this claim is consistent with the account of human nature provided by other branches of philosophy, but his argument does not depend directly on these.

In this interpretation, Aristotle's approach (in using the ideas of human and divine as ethical norms) can be seen as a more sophisticated version of that of Plato and the Presocratics, as outlined earlier. Although they differ in their specific claims about what counts as 'natural', the thinkers converge in accepting that their accounts will only be fully intelligible to those who are properly prepared, in character as well as knowledge, to understand them. The appeal to 'nature' is not an appeal to an independent, purely 'scientific' standpoint that *anyone* should be capable of adopting.[73]

4. *Stoics and Epicureans*

The idea that 'nature' (like 'reason') has a normative role was a prominent one in Stoic theory. But there has been much debate about precisely what role it played; there is also evidence that its precise role was a subject of debate between Stoic thinkers themselves.[74] On the face of it, the Stoics seem to be saying that, if we study the nature of the universe as a whole, this will serve as a means of guiding our own moral lives. But, as in other Greek theories, the point is significantly less simple (and more credible) than it might seem initially. Indeed, Troels Engberg-Pedersen argues that the Stoic claim is, essentially, that human beings are naturally capable of a certain kind of development in ethical understanding, that which consists in moving from ethical subjectivity to objectivity. The Stoic claim is not, essentially, about the character of the natural *kosmos*; nor is it a claim about the role of understanding the *kosmos* in ethical development.[75] Engberg-Pedersen's view may go too far in de-emphasizing the significance of the idea of 'nature' for the Stoics. But the Stoics, like other Greek thinkers, stress that understanding the normative significance of 'nature' depends on developing the kind of character and state of mind that corresponds to what is 'natural'.

Julia Annas, following an important article by Jacques Brunschwig, underlines the importance of (one version of) the normal order for studying the branches of knowledge in the Stoic curriculum: first logic or dialectic, then ethics, then physics (the latter signifying the study of nature, including theology).[76] She also stresses that, although the Stoics identify the overall goal of life with 'life according to nature' (or 'according to virtue/reason'), specific Stoic ethical principles are not explicitly based on specific claims about the natural world. The key Stoic ethical claim that virtue is the only good (in comparison with which, all other so-called 'goods' are 'matters of indifference') is presented, as it is by Aristotle, as an independent claim about the nature of happiness.[77] The Stoics do not, Annas believes, set out to *prove*, scientifically (by reference to the facts of nature) that the life based on the idea that virtue is the only good is a 'natural' one, and thus persuade people to become virtuous. The Stoics believe that human beings (unless corrupted by false beliefs encountered in the course of their upbringing)[78] are naturally adapted to develop in a way that leads them to see that virtue is the only good. They also believe that human beings are naturally adapted to develop other-benefiting motivation. Parental love is the classic example of this; but, if fully developed, this inclination will lead to the desire to benefit other human beings as such, whether or not they are directly related to oneself. These are two key features of the Stoic theory of *oikeiōsis* ('familiarization' or 'appropriation').[79] The philosophical study of ethics, following logic or dialectic, builds on (and advances) this process of development, by enabling people to understand the principles involved in this process. But the aim of ethical philosophy is not, Annas argues, to initiate this process by proving that it is natural by reference to an analysis of the *kosmos*.[80] Other recent accounts give a rather more important role than Annas does to the idea of 'nature' in motivating people towards virtue and in providing a pattern of rationality to guide people to lead (normatively) 'rational' lives.[81] But they do not, I think, deny her claim that, to be effective, the idea of 'nature' must answer to the ethical agent's understanding of what is 'natural'. This depends, first, on the agent's own ethical development, and then on her ability to grasp the key principles of Stoic ethical philosophy.

It is at the third stage ('physics') that the Stoics do analyse cosmic nature, seeing here, like Plato in the *Timaeus*, the evidence of providential rationality and order. 'God', for the Stoics, is an immanent (rather than separate or 'transcendent') force in nature, identical with providential rationality and order.[82] Human beings, alone among animals, are constitutively capable of using their rationality to recognize this rationality in the universe.[83] The ideal outcome of this stage is that one can connect the account given of the natural *kosmos* both with the key principles of ethical philosophy and with one's own ethical experience and development. At this point, one will understand, in the fullest possible way, what it means to say that 'the life according to virtue' is also 'the life according to nature'. Such an understanding will complete and enhance one's grasp of the key ethical principles; but it would seem that, for most Stoic thinkers at least, it does not introduce any substantively new principles.[84] On this point, there is a partial difference between the Stoics and some earlier thinkers. For Plato and Aristotle, as we saw in Ch. III, post-reflective understanding leads one to revise one's view of the highest possible human happiness, identifying this, ultimately, with philosophical knowledge rather than practical, other-benefiting action. For the Stoics, such action, if performed in the best possible way, is just as much an exercise of rationality or 'wisdom' as is philosophical knowledge.[85]

Epicurean thinking on this topic is rather different, since Epicurus claims that nature provides the basis for a radical revision of the ethical principles of conventional societies, and that, without this revision, human happiness is unobtainable. The fundamental point is that the proper goal of all human (and animal) desire is pleasure, defined as freedom from physical pain (*aponia*) and freedom from mental and emotional disturbance (*ataraxia*).[86] Epicurus also subdivides desires according to whether they are natural or necessary, both, or neither; those which are neither natural nor necessary are described as based on 'empty belief' (κενοδοξία).[87] On this basis, Epicurus makes a fundamental critique of conventional goals (such as the desire for wealth and social or political status), and of the emotions, especially anger, which are based on false beliefs such as that retaliation is a good thing.[88] Also, whereas the Stoics present parental love as a basic human (and animal) instinct,[89] Epicurus thinks that all forms of interpersonal and communal relationship should be chosen by reference to the overall goal of the life of pleasure. Friendship between those whose lives are directed by Epicurean objectives emerges as the most important type of relationship and one in which pleasure can be achieved most reliably.[90]

Whereas, for the Stoics, as interpreted earlier, the study of cosmic nature builds on ethical philosophy (and on ethical development at the practical level), the study of nature is an integral part of Epicurean philosophical activity throughout.[91] However, on this point a paradox seems to emerge, which Martha Nussbaum has underlined. On the one hand, Epicurus stresses that 'nature' (as he analyses this) constitutes the basis for guiding ethical life. On the other, he stresses that the ultimate goal of scientific activity is to secure peace of mind. He also claims that, on many points, alternative scientific explanations are acceptable, provided that they are compatible with the account of the natural world that, as Epicurus thinks, provides the basis for peace of mind (one that is framed in purely naturalistic terms, without reference to divine intervention).[92] Nussbaum also couples with this point some evidence that Epicurus and his followers practised forms of doctrinal and emotional indoctrination, rather than encouraging open-minded, critical debate, as other Greek philosophical schools did. She takes this as an indication that the Epicureans interpreted in a very literal way the prevalent Greek idea that philosophy was a type of 'therapy' for emotions and desires: the 'curative' goal of the therapy was given priority over the critical examination of the truths about nature on which this therapy was allegedly based.[93]

However, it is possible to read this evidence rather differently. Epicurus' point may be, rather, that his account of nature serves the overall goal of achieving pleasure precisely because it is true (and that it could not do so unless it were true). Alternative explanations of natural phenomena are acceptable, but if, and only if, they are consistent with an explanatory framework that is itself well-grounded. Also, the stress on the 'rehearsal' of Epicurus' teachings, and the absorption (or 'internalization')[94] of their ethical implications need not be taken as a form of conditioning or 'brainwashing'. It may be taken, instead, as the equivalent of the idea that we have met in other Greek theories: that there needs to be a match between the state of mind and character of the learner and the account of nature being offered, if the ethical implications of this account are to be understood fully.[95]

The latter point comes out in one of the most problematic features of Epicurean thinking, that relating to the nature of the gods. While maintaining that the gods exist, and that they are, broadly, as human beings suppose them to be, Epicurus insists that the gods play no role in the creation or direction of the natural world, which is wholly intelligible by reference to natural laws. The precise nature of the (physical or quasi-physical) existence and location of the gods seems to have been a matter of debate even among Epicureans as well as a target for criticism by non-Epicureans.[96] A radical new theory about Epicurus' thinking on this has been advanced by Long and Sedley. They believe that the gods are, for Epicurus, in essence, the product of human thoughts (since Epicurus is a thoroughgoing materialist, this is not to deny the gods a certain kind of physical existence). However, in their account, Epicurus also thinks that there are true and false beliefs about the gods, and that the true beliefs are those which are consistent with the true (Epicurean) account of the nature of the universe and about the ideal life (which the gods exemplify), that of complete freedom from pain and disturbance.[97] Whether or not their view is correct, there is one feature of Epicurean thinking on this topic which is especially relevant to this chapter. This is that, for Epicurus, the true nature of the gods is only properly intelligible to those human beings who think about them with the right state of mind and character, one which matches the gods' peace of mind and freedom from false beliefs and desires. For those who approach them in this spirit, 'worship' of the gods (whatever precisely this means for Epicureans) can help to instil correct understanding of the ethical ideal, as well as helping them to form a true conception of the natural order. As Lucretius puts it (in language which also reflects Epicurus' views), 'piety' does not inhere in the usual religious rituals but rather in 'contemplating the nature of everything with a peaceful mind'.[98]

I close this chapter by returning to the issue raised at the start about the relationship between Greek and modern thinking about 'nature' as a normative idea. I noted that MacIntyre and Williams believe that Aristotle's thinking of this topic represents a valid type of theorizing, though they have reservations, for different reasons, about the idea that this type of thinking can be transferred to the modern intellectual situation.[99] MacIntyre and Williams recognize that Aristotle is not claiming (implausibly) that a study of the bare facts of nature should be enough to persuade *anyone*, whatever her character, that she has reason to be ethically good.[100] This chapter underlines this point, as regards Aristotle, and extends it to other Greek thinkers of different periods. The Greek thinkers explore, in different ways, the idea that full understanding of the ethical implications of nature depends on the person concerned developing the kind of character that matches those ethical implications. Different Greek thinkers give differing weight to the role of philosophy (as distinct from practical life and interpersonal and communal relationships) in developing this kind of character; but all of them give some weight to philosophy in this process.[101] Although the Greek theories discussed differ on this point as well as on others, I think that Greek thought on this subject is both more credible and more subtle that is often supposed, and that some of the recent work cited can help to bring out this point.

The question whether this kind of thinking is also a conceptual possibility for us today falls outside the scope of this kind of book; but it is worth making some general points. For modern thinkers, as noted earlier, it is tempting to supply the kind of intellectual framework familiar from the history of Western thought, in which the Christian world-view has traditionally been taken to ground a certain moral framework, one that has also achieved widespread currency in conventional ethical thinking. As noted earlier (text to nn. 16–19 above), Greek thinkers operate against a very different religious and intellectual background. A further difference between Greek and modern conditions is that, for Plato and Aristotle at least, full ethical and intellectual development does not yield a wholly 'harmonious' picture of human nature, as Williams suggests regarding Aristotle, but rather one that accepts the competing claims of practical and contemplative wisdom.[102] Also, for virtually all the Greek thinkers discussed, the outcome of reflective thought (including thought about the ethical significance of 'nature') is to generate *some* conflict with conventional ethical thought. Although these points mark in some ways a difference from the traditional background of modern thinking on ethics and nature, they also bring out the complexity and sophistication of Greek thought in these respects. In the contemporary Western intellectual context, where there is no generally accepted religio-ethical world-view, the line of thought pursued by the Greek thinkers may strike modern readers as more credible than they would have expected.

NOTES

1. The title of this chapter is also that of a book on a related topic: M. Schofield and G. Striker, edd., *The Norms of Nature: Studies in Hellenistic Ethics* (Cambridge, 1986).

2. i.e. those of normative rationality (Ch. II), of ethical motivation (Ch. III), of the virtuous community (Ch. IV).

3. Obvious examples are the controversies about the ideas of Galileo and Darwin. A recent development is the emergence of thinkers who argue, by contrast, that a Christian world-view is fully compatible with current scientific thinking: see e.g. J. Polkinghorne, *Science and Christian Belief* (London, 1994).

4. However, Kant saw this as a function of our existence as purely rational ('noumenal') beings,

as distinct from our existence as members of the natural world and as subject to natural laws. See Kant, in H. J. Paton, *The Moral Law* (London, 1986), pp. 107–20; for analysis, see e.g. T. Irwin, 'Morality and Personality: Kant and Green', in A. W. Wood, ed., *Self and Nature in Kant's Philosophy* (Ithaca, 1984), pp. 31–56.

5. On the 'prisoner's dilemma', see e.g. R. D. Luce and H. Raiffa, *Games and Decisions* (New York, 1957); R. Axelrod, *The Evolution of Cooperation* (Harmondsworth, 1984). On the 'veil of ignorance', see J. Rawls, *A Theory of Justice* (Cambridge, Mass., 1971). For the claim that a proper understanding of rationality or personal identity should lead one to see that it is rational to be morally good (i.e. motivated to benefit others), see A. Gewirth, *Reason and Morality* (Chicago, 1977); D. Parfit, *Reasons and Persons* (Oxford, 1984), esp. part 3.

6. See A. MacIntyre, *After Virtue* (London, 1985, 2nd edn.), chs. 4–7; B. Williams, *Ethics and the Limits of Philosophy* (London, 1985), pp. 54–70, 77–81; on Parfit's work, see Williams, *Moral Luck* (Cambridge, 1981), ch., 1.

7. See Williams, *Ethics and the Limits of Philosophy*, pp. 30–4. However, various features of *R.*, including the idea that the full development of virtue requires a complex two-stage process in a reason-ruled *polis*, are not compatible with the idea that arguments can persuade *anyone* to be just; see Ch. IV, text to nn. 57–62, and see further C. Gill, *Personality in Greek Epic, Tragedy, and Philosophy* (Oxford, 1996), 6.6. For discussions of the central argument about justice in Pl. *R.*, see Ch. IV, n. 55.

8. See MacIntyre, *After Virtue*, ch. 12, taken with chs. 14–15; also *Whose Justice? Which Rationality?* (London, 1988), chs. 6–7.

9. See Williams, *Ethics and the Limits of Philosophy*, ch. 3, esp. pp. 43–7, 51–3.

10. Williams, *Ethics and the Limits of Philosophy*, pp. 51–3 (cf. 43–4), and MacIntyre, *After Virtue*, pp. 148, 158, adopt versions of the former view; for discussion, see C. Gill, 'The Human Being as an Ethical Norm', in Gill, ed., *The Person and the Human Mind: Issues in Ancient and Modern Philosophy* (Oxford, 1990), pp. 137–61, esp. pp. 138–43, 152–5. MacIntyre adopts the second view in his review of Gill, ed., *Person and Human Mind*, in *Arion* (3rd series) 1 (1991), 188–94, esp. pp. 191–2, cited in text to n. 11 below. See also MacIntyre, *Whose Justice? Which Rationality?*, chs. 7–8.

11. Williams, *Ethics and the Limits of Philosophy*, p. 52; MacIntyre, review of Gill, ed., *Person and Human Mind*, p. 192. In *Whose Justice? Which Rationality?*, pp. 141–5, MacIntyre acknowledges the tension apparently created in Aristotle's account of virtue and happiness by *NE* 10. 7–8 (on which, see Ch. III, text to nn. 72–81), but argues that this does not undermine the fundamental cohesion (or harmony) of Aristotle's world-view.

12. See J. McDowell, review of Williams, *Ethics and the Limits of Philosophy*, Mind 95 (1986), 377–86; see also his 'The Role of *Eudaimonia* in Aristotle's *Ethics*', in A. O. Rorty, ed., *Essays on Aristotle's Ethics* (Berkeley, 1980), pp. 359–76, esp. pp. 366–73; J. Annas, 'Naturalism in Greek Ethics: Aristotle and After', *Proceedings of the Boston Area Colloquium* 4 (1988), 149–71; Gill, 'The Human Being as an Ethical Norm', pp. 137–61, esp. pp. 138–43, 152–5; also Gill, *Personality*, 6. 4–5; M. C. Nussbaum, 'Aristotle on Human Nature and the Foundation of Ethics', in J. E. G. Altham and R. Harrison, edd., *World, Mind and Ethics: Essays on the Philosophy of Bernard Williams* (Cambridge, forthcoming).

13. See Gill, *Personality*, 6. 5, text to nn. 130–2, taken with 4. 6–7, 5. 6–7. For a different type of 'instability' in Aristotle's ethical viewpoint, see J. Annas, *Morality of Happiness* (Oxford, 1993), ch. 18.

14. *Morality of Happiness*, part 2, esp. chs. 3, 9.

15. For the criticism by Williams and MacIntyre of this move in modern philosophy, see text to n. 6 above. For certain significant variations in the way in which this shared approach is applied by Greek thinkers, see nn. 59, 101 below.

16. See e.g. *Il.* 24. 527–33 (Achilles on the two jars on the threshold of Zeus), cited, significantly, by Plato in his critique of traditional theology in *R.* 2 (379d). See also n. 19 below. For tragic statements about the problematic ethical status of the gods, see e.g. Sophocles, *Trachiniae* 1264–78, Euripides, *Hippolytus* 120, *Herakles* 1313–46.

17. Prominent critics of traditional poetic theology were Xenophanes and Plato (e.g. *R.* 377d–383b); for redefinitions of the divine, see e.g. D. E. Rice and J. E. Stambaugh, *Sources for the Study of Greek Religion* (Missoula, Montana, 1979), pp. 44–50; also J. Bremmer, *Greek Religion* (Oxford, 1994), pp. 12, 89–90.

18. This is not to deny that such speculation could lead to conflict with conventional ideas about religion and its ethical implications; see text to nn. 40–3 below.

19. A different picture from that offered in this paragraph is given by H. Lloyd-Jones, *The Justice of Zeus* (Berkeley, 1971): Lloyd-Jones argues that the idea of god (esp. Zeus) as an objective moral arbiter

is prominent in Greek literature and thought from the *Iliad* onwards, and suggests that the later Greek philosophical idea of the *kosmos* as a providentially ordered whole can be seen as a linear continuation of the religious view. But I think that there are substantial difficulties in Lloyd-Jones's view, one of which has been underlined by N. Yamagata, in *Homeric Morality* (Leiden, 1994). Although Homeric poetry sometimes presents human beings as believing that the gods serve as impartial moral arbiters, the gods themselves are characteristically presented as activated by their concern for their own honour, their own favourites, or by the constraints of fate (*moira*); see her Part 1, esp. pp. 1–2, and ch. 6. Also important is R. Parker's suggestion that the ethics of reciprocity (not of impartial or disinterested justice) constitute the relevant framework for thinking about the morality of Greek gods; see 'Reciprocity in Greek Religion', in C. Gill, N. Postlethwaite, R. Seaford, edd., *Reciprocity in Ancient Greece* (Oxford, forthcoming).

20. Two other features bearing on the interpretation of the Presocratics have been brought out by recent studies: the importance of placing the Presocratics in their largely oral culture, dominated by poetic modes of expression: see E. A. Havelock, 'The Linguistic Task of the Presocratics', in K. Robb, ed. *Language and Thought in Early Greek Philosophy* (La Salle, Illinois, 1983); the importance of locating the 'fragments' of the Presocratics in the context of the writings that quote or comment on them, including highly partisan early Christian writers: see C. Osborne, *Rethinking Early Greek Philosophy* (London, 1987). Both points have possible implications for the question being pursued here.

21. The standard source-book for the Presocratics is H. Diels, *Die Fragmente der Vorsokratiker*, rev. W. Kranz, 2 vols. (Berlin, 1961, 10th edn.) (=DK); all fragments cited below are as numbered in DK, and are B fragments (frs.) unless otherwise specified. See also G. S. Kirk, J. E. Raven, and M. Schofield, *The Presocratic Philosophers* (Cambridge, 1983, 2nd edn.); M. R. Wright, *The Presocratics*, main fragments with introduction and commentary (Bristol, 1985); both books contain useful bibliographies. Some at least of the points made here could also have been made in connection with e.g. Anaximander (for whom 'justice' is both a cosmic and a normative principle) and Parmenides (for whom the recognition of the unity of being transforms both the understanding of nature and that of human knowledge and aspiration). See e.g. Anaximander, fr. A9, Parmenides frs. 1–2, 6–8; see further C. H. Kahn, *Anaximander and the Origins of Greek Cosmology* (New York, 1960); A. P. D. Mourelatos, *The Route of Parmenides* (New Haven, 1970).

22. See esp. frs. 1, 2, 26, 41, 50, 54, 67, 117–18, 123; see Kirk, Raven, Schofield, *Presocratic Philosophers*, ch. 6; C. H. Kahn, *The Art and Thought of Heraclitus* (Cambridge, 1979); E. Hussey, 'Epistemology and Meaning in Heraclitus', in M. Schofield and M. C. Nussbaum, edd., *Language and Logos: Studies in Ancient Greek Philosophy Presented to G. E. L. Owen* (Cambridge, 1982), pp. 33–59.

23. M. R. Wright, 'Presocratic Minds', in Gill, ed., *Person and Human Mind*, pp. 207–25, quotation from p. 221; see also her pp. 218–25.

24. See esp. fr. 101: 'I searched out myself'; also Kirk, Raven, Schofield, *Presocratic Philosophers*, pp. 211–12. On the possible influence of the mystery cults on Presocratics such as Heraclitus, see R. Seaford, 'Immorality, Salvation, and the Elements', *Harvard Studies in Classical Philology* 90 (1986), 1–26; see esp. pp. 14–20.

25. My account follows that of M. R. Wright, *Empedocles: The Extant Fragments*, ed. with introduction and commentary (New Haven, 1981), esp. pp. 57–76; also Kirk, Raven, Schofield, *Presocratic Philosophers*, ch. 10, esp. pp. 320–1. For other interpretations, see Wright, p. 57 n. 1; also Kirk, Raven, Schofield, p. 459.

26. See esp. frs. 6, 17 (esp. lines 21–6), 27, 29, 31, 105, 109, 133–4. See also Wright, *Empedocles*, pp. 72–5.

27. The process is couched partly in terms of transmigration of lives, e.g. frs. 115, 137. Although Empedocles' thought can be interpreted in analytic terms, as summarized here, it may also be seen as based on religious practices, such as those linked with the mystery cults; see e.g. G. Zuntz, *Persephone* (Oxford, 1971), pp. 181–274; Seaford, 'Immortality, Salvation, and the Elements', 10–14.

28. See esp. frs. 121, 130, 136; 110 (line 2 cited).

29. This point anticipates a theme discussed earlier in later Greek ethical thought: that the best possible way to benefit others is to communicate to them what is taken to be the truth (esp. about the nature of human happiness), even if the truth so conveyed does not consist in the recommendation of what is conventionally taken to be other-benefiting virtue; see Ch. III, text to nn. 78–81.

30. Pythagoras himself wrote nothing; and the earliest evidence for Pythagorean number-theory comes from Philolaus (5th c.), to whom some scholars, including Burkert, attribute key features of the theory. On this question, see Kirk, Raven, Schofield, *Presocratic Philosophers*, pp. 215–16, 324, also chs.

7, 11; W. Burkert, *Lore and Science in Ancient Pythagoreanism* (Cambridge, Mass., 1972); C. H. Kahn, 'Pythagorean Philosophy before Plato', in A. P. D. Mourelatos, *The Pre-Socratics: A Collection of Critical Essays* (New York, 1974), pp. 161–85; C. A. Huffman, *Philolaus of Croton: Pythagorean and Presocratic* (Cambridge, 1993).

31. See esp. Kirk, Raven, Schofield, *Presocratic Philosophers*: Pythagoras frs. 269–72, 275, 277, 285–6; Philolaus, frs. 450–8, (fr. nos. as in Kirk, Raven, Schofield).

32. This is not because the Presocratics were wholly naive regarding philosophical methodology. Scholars have, for a long time, presumed that the history of Presocratic philosophy consisted in a continuing debate about ideas of nature and, to some extent, about philosophical methodology: on the latter, see e.g. T. Irwin, *Classical Thought* (Oxford, 1989), pp. 29–38. But they seem not to have discussed explicitly the issues raised by linking the study of nature and ethics in this way.

33. As with other aspects of intellectual life in this period, it is difficult to draw a clear line between Plato and the late fifth-century intellectual debates for which he is such an important, but partisan, source. For attempts to gain a historical perspective on this period that is not unduly shaped by Plato, see e.g. E. A. Havelock, *The Liberal Temper in Greek Politics* (London, 1957); C. Farrar, *The Origins of Democratic Thought: The Invention of Politics in Classical Athens* (Cambridge, 1988); J. de Romilly, *The Great Sophists in Periclean Athens* (Oxford, 1992).

34. W. K. C. Guthrie, *A History of Greek Philosophy* (=*HGP*), vol. 3 (Cambridge, 1969), chs. 4–5, discusses a wide range of sources; G. B. Kerferd, *The Sophistic Movement* (Cambridge, 1981), ch. 10, offers a more analytic account.

35. See Guthrie, *HGP*, vol. 3, pp. 101–16; Kerferd, *Sophistic Movement*, pp. 115–23 (also discussing Thrasymachus in Plato *R.* 1); for Callicles, see Pl. *Gorgias* 481 ff., esp. 482–3. The usual view of Antiphon as an 'immoralist' is questioned by T. J. Saunders, 'Antiphon the Sophist on Natural Laws', *Proceedings of the Aristotelian Society* 78 (1977–8), 26–35, but restated by D. Furley in 'Antiphon's Case against Justice', in G. B. Kerferd, ed., *The Sophists and their Legacy* (Wiesbaden, 1981), pp. 81–91.

36. See Guthrie, *HGP*, vol. 3, pp. 84–8, and Kerferd, *Sophistic Movement*, pp. 123–5, referring to e.g. two debates in Thucydides: the Melian debate (esp. 5. 105.2) and the Mitylenean debate (esp. 3.40.4, 44.1.).

37. See Guthrie, *HGP*, vol. 3, pp. 63–79; Kerferd, *Sophistic Movement*, pp. 125–30, referring to e.g. Protagoras and the *Anonymus Iamblichi*. See also Ch. IV, text to nn. 46–7.

38. See Guthrie, *HGP*, vol. 3, ch. 5; Kerferd, *Sophistic Movement*, pp. 147–50, referring to e.g. Pl. *R.* 358e–359b (a position put forward for the sake of the argument), Critias, *Sisyphus* DK fr. 25; for another, more positive, version of the social contract theory, see Pl. *Crito* 50c–53a.

39. On the latter view, see Ch. IV, section 3.

40. For these and other suggestions about cultural and intellectual factors underlying this debate (including responses to the 'naturalism' of the Presocratics), see Irwin, *Classical Thought*, ch. 4, esp. pp. 59–67; Kerferd, *Sophistic Movement*, pp. 112–14, Guthrie, *HGP*, vol. 3, ch. 2.

41. On these thinkers, see e.g. Kirk, Raven, Schofield, *Presocratic Philosophers*, chs. 12, 16; and M. Schofield, *An Essay on Anaxagoras* (Cambridge, 1980); A. Laks, *Diogène d' Apollonie* (Lille, 1983).

42. See Aristophanes, *Clouds* 366–436, 1075–82, 1399–1405; Pl. *Apology* 18b–19d, 23d–e, 26d–e; *Laws* 888e–890a; see also Guthrie, *HGP*, vol. 3, pp. 113–16.

43. It is clear from Pl. *Ap.* (refs. in n. 42 above) that Plato thought that the popular impression that Socrates had engaged in this kind of speculation had proved very damaging, and had contributed to Socrates' being brought to trial on the charges of 'corrupting the young and not believing in the gods that the city believes in'. For recent discussions of Socrates' trial and of his 'piety', see Ch. IV, text to nn. 37–43.

44. Plato's dialogues are usually subdivided into early (supposedly recreating the dialectical mode of the early Socrates); middle (supposedly developing independent metaphysical theories); late (either re-examining these theories or taking them further). *Phaedo* is usually classed (like *R.*) as 'middle', *Timaeus* as 'late'. On Plato's chronology, see L. Brandwood, 'Stylometry and Chronology', in R. Kraut, ed., *The Cambridge Companion to Plato* (Cambridge, 1992), pp. 90–120. On Plato's use of the dialogue form, see refs. in Ch. IV, n. 40.

45. See *Phaedo* 96a–99c, esp. 97b–98c; for Socrates' application of his alternative approach to what is, in a sense, the 'natural world', see 100a–106e. See further D. Gallop, *Plato*: Phaedo, tr. with commentary (Oxford, 1975); D. Bostock, *Plato's* Phaedo (Oxford, 1986); C. J. Rowe, *Plato*: Phaedo, ed. with introduction and commentary (Cambridge, 1993).

46. For a succinct statement of the relationship between *Phaedo* and *Timaeus*, see T. Irwin,

Classical Thought (Oxford, 1989), pp. 111–13. See e.g. *Timaeus* 35b–36d, 38c–39e, 43a–47e, 53c–57c. On the *Timaeus*, see e.g. G. Vlastos, *Plato's Universe* (Oxford, 1975), chs. 2–3; Guthrie, *HGP*, vol. 5, ch. 4 (see his index under 'Pythagoreans').

47. *Phaedo* 68c–69c, 78d–79d, 82e–84a. Conventional virtue is conceived simply as the exchange of one body-based pleasure and pain for another. For the idea that real virtue depends on philosophical reflection or dialectic, see Ch. III, text to n. 38, also nn. 69–70. On the possible influence of the mystery cults on Plato's use, here and elsewhere, of ideas such as 'purification', see C. Riedweg, *Mysterienter- minologie bei Platon, Philon und Klemens von Alexandrien* (Berlin, 1987).

48. See *Timaeus* 42e–47d, 69d–72d, 86b–89e; on the idea that certain vices depend on defective physiological make-up (86b–87b), see M. M. Mackenzie, *Plato On Punishment* (Berkeley, 1981), pp. 176–8; on the psychology of the *Timaeus*, see T. M. Robinson, *Plato's Psychology* (Toronto, 1970), chs. 4–5.

49. See *Timaeus* 47b–d, 90a–d, taken with 44b–c, 87b; i.e. Plato is not saying that the *bare facts* of nature can make *anyone* good, regardless of her pre-existing character; on the relevant issue, see text to n. 15 above.

50. See Ch. III, text to nn. 67–71.

51. *R.* 529a–530e; on this combination of types of knowledge, see e.g. I. Mueller, 'Mathematical Method and Philosophical Truth', in Kraut, ed., *Cambridge Companion to Plato*, pp. 170–99, esp. pp. 183–94.

52. See T. Irwin, *Plato's Moral Theory* (Oxford, 1977), ch. 7, esp. pp. 230–48; *Plato's Ethics* (Oxford, 1995), chs. 17–18; see further Ch. III, text to nn. 62–3, and Gill, *Personality*, 4.3, 5.2.

53. See *R.* 500a–501c, esp. 500c–d, taken with 400d–402c, esp. 401d–402c.

54. See H.-J. Krämer, *Arete bei Platon und Aristoteles* (Heidelberg, 1959, 2nd edn. Amsterdam, 1967); also K. Gaiser, *Platons Ungeschriebene Lehre* (Stuttgart, 1968, 2nd edn.); J. N. Findlay, *Plato: The Written and Unwritten Doctrines* (London, 1974); scholars presently pursuing this approach include T. Szlezák and G. Reale. For a succinct account, see Gaiser, 'Plato's Enigmatic Lecture on the Good', *Phronesis* 25 (1980), 1–37; and, for a review of the whole subject, see *Methexis* 6 (1993), a special issue on Plato's unwritten doctrines.

55. See e.g. G. Vlastos's famous critique of Krämer, *Arete*, 'On Plato's Oral Doctrine', in *Platonic Studies* (2nd edn., Princeton, 1981), pp. 379–403. See also K. M. Sayre, *Plato's Late Ontology: A Riddle Resolved* (Princeton, 1983), who sees the unwritten doctrines as virtually identical with the ideas of Plato's *Philebus*.

56. M. F. Burnyeat, 'Platonism and Mathematics: A Prelude to Discussion', in A. Graeser, ed., *Mathematics and Metaphysics in Aristotle: Proceedings of the X Symposium Aristotelicum* (Bern/ Stuttgart, 1987), pp. 213–40; esp. pp. 217–20, 232–40.

57. See e.g. *Timaeus* 35a–36d, 43a–44a, 54c–56c; see further text to nn. 48–9 above.

58. On the two-stage programme of ethical education in *R.*, see Ch. III, text to nn. 67–71; on relevant refs. in *R.*., see n. 53 above.

59. For the Presocratics, see text to nn. 21–31 above; see also text to n. 47 above, nn. 86–90, 94–5 below, on comparable positions in Pl. *Phaedo* and Epicurean philosophy. For the Aristotelian and (one version of the) Stoic position, which stress rather, like Pl. *R.*, the importance of *pre-reflective* character-development as a preliminary for reflective understanding of the role of nature, see text to nn. 67, 78–9 below. This broad division in Greek thought represents part of the division noted in Ch. III, text to n. 38; see also n. 101 below.

60. Roughly speaking, ethics is characterized by (1) its practical rather than theoretical aim; (2) its focus on the question of the proper overall goal of a human life; (3) the importance of the notion of virtue (including virtue of character, *ēthos*, the term which gives 'ethics', *ēthica*, its name). See e.g. *NE* 1. 1, 13, 2. 1–2. See further Annas, *Morality of Happiness*, chs. 1–2; also C. Gill, 'Ethical Thought, Classical', in D. Zeyl, ed., *Encyclopedia of Classical Philosophy* (New York, forthcoming).

61. M. C. Nussbaum, *The Fragility of Goodness* (Cambridge, 1986), chs. 8 and 10; on the Platonic approach, see her ch. 5.

62. J. Lear, *Aristotle: The Desire to Understand* (Cambridge, 1988), esp. chs. 1, 4, and 6. 8; see esp. *Metaphysics* 12. 7, 9, *De Anima* (*On the Soul*) 3. 3–5, taken with *NE* 10. 7, 1177b26–1178a22. A distinct, but partly parallel, approach is taken by T. Irwin, in *Aristotle's First Principles* (Oxford, 1988): he thinks that Aristotle believes that 'strong dialectic' (argument based on unrefutable metaphysical principles) can provide the basis for conclusions about the issues of other branches of philosophy, including ethics.

63. Other important texts for this question include the characterization of 'what each of us is' (i.e. our essential human nature) in the discussion of friendship, *NE* 9. 4, esp. 1166a13–23, 9. 8, esp. 1168b28–1169a3 (see Ch. III, text to n. 45). See also the analysis of *akrasia* ('weakness of will') 'in a way that makes reference to nature', φυσικῶς (*NE* 7. 3, esp. 1147a24–5); and the analysis of the role of friendship in happiness 'in a way that makes *more* reference to nature' (than the preceding arguments), φυσικώτερον (*NE* 9. 9, 1170a13–14).

64. See text to nn. 8–11 above; for the idea of 'metaphysical biology', see MacIntyre, *After Virtue*, p. 148.

65. See refs in n. 12 above.

66. See text to nn. 8–9, 12 above. On the idea of an 'Archimedean point', a fulcrum or pivotal point, that should persuade *anyone*, regardless of her pre-existing beliefs or character, see Williams, *Ethics and the Limits of Philosophy*, ch. 2 (Williams himself regards this idea as illusory).

67. See *NE* 1. 3–4, esp. 1095b6–7, 10. 9, esp. 1179b4–31; see M. F. Burnyeat, 'Aristotle on Learning to be Good', in A. O. Rorty, ed., *Essays on Aristotle's* Ethics (Berkeley, 1980), pp. 69–92, esp. pp. 71–6.

68. *NE* 1. 7 includes a brief survey of the relationship between human and non-human capacities, 1097b33–1098a5; on his views elsewhere on distinctively human capacities, see e.g. C. Gill, 'Is There a Concept of Person in Greek Philosophy?', in S. Everson, ed., *Psychology: Companions to Ancient Thought 2* (Cambridge, 1991), pp. 166–93, esp. pp. 171–84; R. Sorabji, *Animal Minds and Human Morals: The Origins of the Western Debate* (London, 1993), esp. Part 1.

69. The key passage in *NE* 1. 7 (1098a7–18), arguably, has a different function in the argument from that of 10. 7–8, namely that of giving an 'outline' (for this idea, see 1098a20–2) of an account of happiness (see esp. a17–18, 'if there are several types of virtue, in accordance with the best and most perfect type'), whereas 10. 7–8 adjudicates between the most serious candidates for the role of being 'best and most perfect'.

70. See Ch. III, text to nn. 72–81.

71. See refs. in n. 62 above; also *NE* 6. 7, esp. 1141a18–b12, 6. 12, esp. 1144a1–6, 6. 13, esp. 1145a6–11.

72. See further Gill, *Personality*, 5. 6.

73. For this, as a general feature of Greek thinking, see n. 15 above; for a division between those who do or do not give an important role to *pre-reflective* virtue, see n. 59 above.

74. See A. A. Long and D. N. Sedley, *The Hellenistic Philosophers* (Cambridge, 1987) (=LS), 63 A–C.

75. T. Engberg-Pedersen, 'Discovering the Good: *oikeiōsis and kathēkonta* in Stoic Ethics', in Schofield and Striker, edd., *Norms of Nature*, pp. 145–83; 'Stoic Ethics and the Concept of a Person', in Gill, ed., *Person and Human Mind*, pp. 109–35; *The Stoic Theory of* Oikeiosis: *Moral Development and Social Interaction in Early Stoic Theory* (Aarhus, 1990). For a contrasting account, which is more teleological in approach than Engberg-Pedersen's, see N. P. White, 'The Basis of Stoic Ethics', *Harvard Studies in Classical Philology* 83 (1979), 143–78.

76. Annas, *Morality of Happiness*, ch. 5, esp. pp. 163–6; her aim is to reconstruct the view of Chrysippus, the most important and systematic of Stoic thinkers. See also J. Brunschwig, 'On a Book-Title by Chrysippus: "On the Fact that the Ancients Admitted Dialectic along with Demonstrations"', *OSAP* supp. vol. (1991), pp. 81–96. On the Stoic philosophical curriculum, see LS 26 B (different Stoic thinkers held different views about the proper order of the subjects).

77. On this claim and other key Stoic ethical claims, see LS 58, 70.

78. This is (part of) Chrysippus' explanation for the fact that most people fail to complete what he sees as the 'natural' course of ethical development; see Gal. *PHP* (for full ref. see Ch. II, n. 36) V 5. 13–14, pp. 318–21 De Lacy. See further A. A. Long, 'The Stoic Concept of Evil', *Philosophical Quarterly* 18 (1968), 329–42. On the different strands of Stoic thought about the proper context for virtuous social life and development, see Ch. IV, text to nn. 88–94.

79. See LS 59D, 57F: = Cicero, *Fin.* 3. 17, 20–2, 62–8; for a useful edn. of *Fin.* 3, see M. R. Wright, *Cicero: On Stoic Good and Evil*: De Finibus *3 and* Paradoxa Stoicorum, ed. with tr. and commentary (Warminster, 1991). See further G. Striker, 'The Role of *Oikeiosis* in Stoic Ethics', *OSAP* 1 (1983), 145–67; also S. Pembroke, '*Oikeiosis*', in A. A. Long, ed., *Problems in Stoicism* (London, 1971), pp. 114–49.

80. Annas, *Morality of Happiness*, ch. 5, esp. pp. 160–3, 165–75; see also, Gill, 'The Human Being as an Ethical Norm', in Gill, ed., *Person and Human Mind*, esp. pp. 143–51.

81. See e.g. N. P. White, 'Nature and Regularity in Stoic Ethics', *OSAP* 3 (1985), 289–305; G. Striker, 'Following Nature: A Study in Stoic Ethics', *OSAP* 9 (1991), 1–73. On the idea of 'reason' as a norm as well as a function, see Ch. II, text to n. 29.

82. See LS 54; an important source is Cicero, *De Natura Deorum (On the Nature of the Gods) (=ND)* 2, which cites Plato's *Timaeus* at 2. 32. On *Timaeus*, see text to nn. 48–9 above; and on links between Platonic and Stoic thought in these respects, see White, 'Basis of Stoic Ethics', 177–8; also D. Sedley, 'Chrysippus on Psychophysical Causality', in J. Brunschwig and M. C. Nussbaum, edd., *Passions and Perceptions* (Cambridge, 1993), pp. 313–31.

83. See Cic. *ND* 2. 133 (=LS 54 N); the line of thought in 2. 133–56 is close to that of *Timaeus* 44d–47e; see also LS 63 D–E. On Stoic thinking on the relationship between human and animal psychological functions and the moral implications of these, see Sorabji, *Animal Minds and Human Morals* (see his index under 'Stoics').

84. On this point, see Annas, *Morality of Happiness*, pp. 165–6; note also the rather stronger role given to the idea of nature in refs. in n. 81 above. Annas suggests that some later Stoics, esp. Epictetus and Marcus Aurelius, do use the idea of cosmic nature to introduce a new ethical principle: that we are 'only a part of the *kosmos*' and that this fact should affect the way that we shape our lives: Annas, pp. 175–9. See further R. B. Rutherford, *The Meditations of Marcus Aurelius: A Study* (Oxford, 1989); the revised Everyman translation of Epictetus' *Discourses* by R. Hard, with introduction by C. Gill (London, 1995); A. A. Long, 'Epictetus and Marcus Aurelius', in J. Luce, ed., *Ancient Writers: Greece and Rome* (New York, 1982), pp. 985–1002, to be reprinted in Long, *Stoic Studies* (Cambridge, forthcoming).

85. See e.g. Cic. *Fin.* 3. 62–8, esp. 64, 65, 68 (=LS 57 F), also LS 66 J. On Stoic thinking about other-benefiting motivation, see Annas, *Morality of Happiness*, pp. 262–76; and, on the question whether Stoic thinking represents an exception to the Greek tendency to define norms of interpersonal ethics in terms of mutual benefit rather than altruism, Gill, 'Reciprocity or Altruism in Greek Ethical Philosophy?', in Gill, Postlethwaite, Seaford, edd., *Reciprocity in Ancient Greece* (Oxford, forthcoming). On the contrasting position of Plato and Aristotle on this point, see Ch. III, section 4.

86. See LS 21, esp. A–B. On the Epicurean claim that the behaviour of animals and young children shows that pleasure is naturally taken as the proper object of desire, see the lucid analysis by J. Brunschwig, 'The Cradle Argument in Epicureanism and Stoicism', in Schofield and Striker, edd., *Norms of Nature*, pp. 113–44, esp. pp. 115–28.

87. A further important distinction is between 'static' pleasures (those in which the human organism is in a stable or optimal state) and 'kinetic' ones (those restoring the organism to a stable state). See LS 21 esp. B, I, J, Q–R; see further J. Gosling and C. C. W. Taylor, *The Greeks on Pleasure* (Oxford, 1982), chs. 18–20, esp. 19; G. Striker, 'Epicurean Hedonism', in Brunschwig and Nussbaum, edd., *Passions and Perceptions*, pp. 3–17.

88. See further Annas, *Morality of Happiness*, pp. 188–200; also D. Fowler, 'Epicurean Anger', in S. Braund and C. Gill, edd., *The Passions in Roman Thought and Literature* (Cambridge, forthcoming). An important text for Epicurean thinking about anger is Philodemus, *Peri Orgēs (On Anger)*, ed. C. Wilke (Leipzig, 1974), G. Indelli (Naples, 1988).

89. See LS 57 D–F; see also M. W. Blundell, 'Parental Love and Stoic Οἰκείωσις', *Ancient Philosophy* 10 (1990), 221–42.

90. On Epicurean thinking on friendship, see Ch. III, text to nn. 52–8. On the point that Epicurean thinking, like that of other Greek ethical theories, sets out to define an overall goal for shaping one's life (and not just a system for maximizing localized episodes of pleasure, which is the Cyrenaic strategy), see Annas, *Morality of Happiness*, pp. 334–50, also 227–36, on the Cyrenaics; and M. Hossenfelder, 'Epicurus – Hedonist *malgré lui*', in Schofield and Striker, edd., *Norms of Nature*, pp. 245–63.

91. This point is very clear from Lucretius' account of Epicurean theory, encapsulated in the recurrent idea that 'the terror and darkness of the mind' can only be removed by *naturae species ratioque* (an understanding of 'the form and intelligibility of nature'), *De Rerum Natura (On the Nature of the Universe)* e.g. 1. 146–8. Epicurus' *Peri Phuseōs (On Nature)* was, evidently, one of Epicurus' largest and most important works, though only fragments survive; for the most comprehensive collection of Epicurus' works, including these fragments, see G. Arrighetti, *Epicuro opere* (Turin, 1960, 2nd edn. 1973).

92. See LS 18 C (= Epicurus, *Letter to Pythocles* 85–8), 18 D (= Lucretius 5. 509–33), taken with LS, vol. 1, pp. 94–6.

93. M. C. Nussbaum, 'Therapeutic Arguments: Epicurus and Aristotle', in Schofield and Striker, edd., *Norms of Nature*, pp. 31–74, esp. pp. 32–53; *The Therapy of Desire: Theory and Practice in Hellenistic Ethics* (Princeton, 1994), ch. 4. An important source for her views is Philodemus, *Peri Parrhēsias* (*On Frankness*).

94. On 'internalization' in ethics, see Ch. III, text to n. 24.

95. I propose to argue for this view of Epicurean thinking elsewhere. On the two versions of this idea that we find in Greek thought, see n. 59 above.

96. A key source is Cic. *ND* 1, esp. 49–50, 103–7; see LS 23; the idea that the gods live in the spaces between the worlds (*intermundia*) seems to be an innovation of the 1st c. B.C., designed to clarify what was left unclear by Epicurus; see LS, vol. 1, p. 149.

97. See LS, vol. 1, pp. 144–9; for refs. to other views, see LS, vol. 2, p. 490, esp. A. J. Festugière, *Epicurus and his Gods* (Eng. tr. Oxford, 1955; 2nd French rev. edn., Paris, 1968); K. Kleve, *Gnosis Theon*, in *Symbolae Osloenses* suppl. vol. 19 (Oslo, 1963); D. Lemke, *Die Theologie Epikurs* (Munich, 1973).

98. See Lucretius 5. 1198–203 (= LS 23 A(4)); also 6. 68–79, esp. 75–8 (= LS 23D); LS 23 B, C(3), E(5), F(3), J, K.

99. See text to nn. 8–11 above.

100. In this respect, Greek theory seems to them more plausible than some modern theories (both Kantian and Utilitarian) which do make this claim. See nn. 6–9 above, and see further Gill, *Personality*, 6. 4–6.

101. Broadly speaking, Plato in *R.*, Aristotle, and the Stoics emphasize the role of practical and social life in developing the necessary type of character (though Plato and Aristotle also think that philosophy can legitimately reshape the character so developed), whereas the Presocratics and Epicurus lay stress rather on the role of philosophy in shaping character; see n. 59 above. For analogous issues in Greek thinking about ethical motivation and about politics (and for further complexities in the positions of Plato and the Stoics), see text to nn. 47–53 above, and Ch. III, text to nn. 38, 67–71, Ch. IV, text to nn. 88–94.

102. On Williams's view, see text to n. 11 above. On the complex outcome of full development for Plato, in *R.*, and Aristotle, see Ch. III, text to nn. 67–81. On the different position reached by the Stoics on this point, see text to n. 85 above.

VI. CONCLUSION

I close this survey by highlighting two themes that have recurred in several chapters. One relates to the question of development within the history of Greek thought, and also to the relationship between Greek and modern thought. Discussing recent scholarship on Greek models of mind and ethics, I have given prominence to criticism of specific types of developmental approach.[1] On all four topics discussed, I have underlined ways in which Greek thinking can be seen as closer to contemporary thinking (though not necessarily to earlier stages of Western thought) than is often supposed.[2] In doing so, I have focused especially on the work of Bernard Williams, coupled on some points with that of Alasdair MacIntyre. In pursuing this line, I am not advocating a return to the (sometimes naïvely) idealizing view of Greek culture and thought that was relatively common in the Victorian Age.[3] Nor am I denying the substantive achievements of the anthropological approach in helping us to place Greek thought in its social context and in promoting an appropriate historical and critical distance between ourselves and the Greeks.[4] But I think that Williams is right to insist that, in setting out to explore the relationship between our thought and that of the Greeks, we should not import an unexamined body of assumptions about what precisely 'we' (moderns) do believe about psychology, ethics, politics, and other such subjects. Ideally, the examination of Greek thought should go hand in hand with the *re*-examination of our own ideas. If it does so, there are reasons to think that, despite important differences in culture and era, Greek thought may emerge as less remote from current concerns and positions than it has sometimes seemed in studies based on the anthropological approach.[5] It may be that, as this work of re-examination continues, rather different types of anthropological accounts (including developmental ones) will emerge. But it is important that they should be based on a more up-to-date picture of current thinking than has sometimes been assumed by developmental accounts.

A second general point is this. In this survey, I have offered a personal account of certain scholarly issues that have arisen in four related areas of Greek thought. It would be foolish, on this limited basis, to try to provide here a general characterization of Greek patterns of thinking, particularly as, on most topics, I have referred to Greek philosophical thinking over a broad time-period, as well as to some parallel features in the thought of

Homeric epic and Greek tragedy. However, it may be worth outlining here a concept that I have used in a forthcoming study of Greek thinking about psychology and ethics.[6] This is the idea that Greek thinking can be characterized as 'objective-participant', rather than 'subjective-individualist' (or 'objective-individualist'), a characterization associated with the image of human beings as 'interlocutors' in three connected types of dialogue.

Three aspects of this idea are relevant here. One, relevant to Chapter II, is the idea that, in Greek thought, human psychology is typically conceived in 'objective' terms (those of the relationship between 'parts' or functions), rather than in terms of the (subjective) self-conscious 'I'.[7] Another, relevant to Chapters III and IV, is the idea that human beings are naturally adapted to form their ethical and political beliefs, attitudes, and motives in and through participation in interpersonal and communal interchange. There is little room in Greek thought, I have suggested, for the various kinds of ethical and political 'individualism' that have played such an important role in modern Western thought.[8] Third, there is the idea that, in seeking the foundations for their psychological, ethical, and political lives, human beings do so through shared, systematic debate with the goal of determining objective principles. This can be contrasted with certain modern conceptions of what is involved in determining normative principles. The aim, in Greek thought, is neither a search for a purely individualistic (or 'subjective-individualist') ethic nor for one which relies merely on inter-subjective agreement. Greek thinking about the idea of 'nature' as a norm (Ch. V) can be taken as one example of this pattern of thought: the ethical significance of 'nature' is a matter of shared, reasoned debate about common truths bearing on the best life for human beings in general.[9]

Some of the issues which have recurred in this book can be understood as arising out of the interplay between the three aspects of this model and the three types of 'discourse' (psychological, social, and dialectical) involved. This is the case, for instance, with the question of the respective roles of participation in interpersonal or communal relationships and of reflective or dialectical debate in shaping virtuous character and in providing the basis for the understanding of normative principles. This issue has arisen in connection with ethical education, and the question of the socio-political context in which proper ethical life and development can occur.[10] A related question, emphasized in Chapter V, is that of the respective roles of these factors in shaping the kind of ethical character that corresponds to what the theories present as the best or 'natural' type of human condition.[11] Readers may or may not find the idea of an 'objective-participant' pattern of thinking illuminating as a way of defining certain salient features of

Greek thought (and also of highlighting certain points of contact with contemporary thought). But, if they do, they may find it a pattern which applies to areas of Greek thought other than those discussed here, such as Greek thinking about the functions of dialectic, and about moral (and other types of) knowledge.[12]

Finally, I would like to emphasize (what may be already obvious) the limited nature of what I have tried to do in this book. My aim has been to discuss recent scholarship in Greek thought in sufficient detail to highlight some of the issues that scholars have found interesting and important and to indicate why they have done so. I have not attempted to provide a comprehensive survey of Greek philosophy as a whole (an ambitious project in itself), let alone one of *both* Greek philosophy *and* related features of Greek poetry. But I hope that those readers for whom this book has served as an introduction to Greek philosophy may be motivated to pursue some of these other areas. I add a bibliographical note which focuses on general works which may be useful for this purpose as well as noting some new editions and translations. I give emphasis to the areas of Greek philosophy covered in this survey but also include some important recent studies in other areas.

NOTES

1. See Ch. II, text to nn. 7–15; Ch. III, text to nn. 10–30.

2. See Ch. IV, text to nn. 7–8; Ch. V, text to nn. 15, 102; also refs. in n. 1 above. For some (brief) suggestions why Greek thought may be closer to contemporary thought than to that of some earlier periods of Western history, see C. Gill, *Personality in Greek Epic, Tragedy, and Philosophy: The Self in Dialogue* (Oxford, 1996), 6. 7, text to nn. 247–54.

3. See e.g. R. Jenkyns, *The Victorians and Ancient Greece* (Oxford, 1980), esp. chs. 5, 9, 10.

4. A further relevant modern discipline is that of 'reception-theory', which studies the interplay between text and audience (including audiences in different cultural contexts): see e.g. R. C. Holub, *Reception Theory: A Critical Introduction* (London, 1984); C. Martindale, *Redeeming the Text: Latin Poetry and the Hermeneutics of Reception* (Cambridge, 1992).

5. See further B. Williams, *Shame and Necessity* (Berkeley, 1993), ch. 1.

6. *Personality* (full ref in n. 2 above), esp. Introd., and 6. 7; see also Ch. III above, text to nn. 36–8.

7. See esp. Ch. II, text to nn. 10–17, 27–8, 32–4.

8. See esp. Ch. III, text to nn. 24–30, 38; Ch. IV, *passim*. This point applies both to the kind of 'objective-individualism' associated with Kant (on which, see Ch. III, text to nn. 5–6) and the more radical 'subjective-individualism' associated with Nietzsche and Sartre, see further Gill, *Personality*, esp. Introd. and 6. 7; also refs. in Ch. IV, nn. 2, 92.

9. Examples of thinkers adopting a 'subjective-individualistic' attitude to the determination of moral norms include, again, Nietzsche and Sartre (refs. in n. 8 above); see further (esp. on the relevance of such ideas to the interpretation of Homer's Achilles), Gill, *Personality*, 2.3,5. For one version of a modern theory based on the idea that truth is 'intersubjective', see D. Davidson, *Inquiries into Truth and Interpretation* (Oxford, 1984). On the contrast between Davidson and Plato in this respect, see T. Scaltsas, 'Socratic Moral Realism: An Alternative Justification', *OSAP* 7 (1989), 129–50.

10. See Ch. III, text to n. 38, also section 4; Ch. IV, text to nn. 10–11, 50–2, 57–62, 79–83, 88–100.

See further Gill, *Personality*, 4.7, 5.7. For related questions about what should count as a 'reasonable' emotional response, see Ch. II, text to nn. 19–25, 29–34, 37–40.

11. See esp. Ch. V, nn. 59, 101.

12. Some related questions are explored in C. Gill, 'Afterword: Dialectic and the Dialogue Form in Late Plato', in C. Gill and M. M. McCabe, edd., *Form and Argument in Late Plato* (Oxford, forthcoming).

BIBLIOGRAPHICAL NOTE ON GREEK PHILOSOPHY

General:

D. Zeyl, ed., *Encyclopedia of Classical Philosophy* (New York, forthcoming).

T. Irwin, *Classical Thought* (Oxford, 1989).

W. K. C. Guthrie, *A History of Greek Philosophy* 6 vols., from the Pre-socratics to Aristotle (Cambridge, 1962–81); vols. 2 (on the later Pre-socratics) and 3 (on the sophists and Socrates) are especially useful.

A. A. Long, *Hellenistic Philosophy* (London, 1974, 2nd edn., Berkeley, 1986).

Branches of Greek Philosophy:

On psychology:

S. Everson, ed., *Psychology: Companions to Ancient Thought 2* (Cambridge, 1991).

C. Gill, ed., *The Person and the Human Mind: Issues in Ancient and Modern Philosophy* (Oxford, 1990).

C. Gill, *Personality in Greek Epic, Tragedy, and Philosophy: The Self in Dialogue* (Oxford, 1996), also on ethics.

A. W. Price, *Mental Conflict* (London, 1995).

R. Sorabji, *Animal Minds and Human Morals: The Origins of the Western Debate* (London 1993), also on ethics.

On ethics:

J. Annas, *The Morality of Happiness* (Oxford, 1993); on Aristotle and Hellenistic philosophy.

M. C. Nussbaum, *The Fragility of Goodness: Luck and Ethics in Greek Tragedy and Philosophy* (Cambridge, 1986).

W. J. Prior, *Virtue and Knowledge: An Introduction to Ancient Greek Ethics* (London, 1991).

B. Williams, *Shame and Necessity* (Berkeley, 1993).

On science, cosmology, medicine:

G. E. R. Lloyd, *The Revolutions of Wisdom: Studies in the Claims and Practice of Ancient Greek Science* (Berkeley, 1987).

J. Longrigg, *Greek Rational Medicine: Philosophy and Medicine from Alcmaeon to the Alexandrians* (London, 1993).

M. R. Wright, *Cosmology in Antiquity* (London, 1995).

Note also the Penguin Classics tr. *Hippocratic Writings*, with introduction by G. E. R. Lloyd (Harmondsworth, 1987).

On dialectic, epistemology, and metaphysics:
M. Burnyeat, *The* Theaetetus *of Plato*, tr. M. J. Levett, with introduction by Burnyeat (pp. 1–241) (Indianapolis, 1990).
S. Everson, ed., *Epistemology: Companions to Ancient Thought 1* (Cambridge, 1990).
G. Fine, *On Ideas* (Oxford, 1993).
M. M. McCabe, *Plato's Individuals* (Princeton, 1994).
G. E. L. Owen, *Logic, Science, and Dialectic* (London, 1986).

Periods of Greek Philosophy:

Presocratics and Sophists:
The standard collection of Greek sources remains H. Diels, *Die Fragmente der Vorsokratiker*, rev. W. Kranz, 2 vols. (Berlin, 1961, 10th edn.).
For a selection of texts, with introduction and commentary, see M. R. Wright, *The Presocratics* (Bristol, 1985).
G. S. Kirk, J. E. Raven, M. Schofield, *The Presocratic Philosophers* (Cambridge, 1983, 2nd edn.) contains key texts, translations, and commentary.
K. Freeman, *Ancilla to the Pre-Socratic Philosophers* (Oxford, 1948), contains a complete translation of Diels-Kranz, including both Presocratics and sophists.
Penguin Classics tr. by J. Barnes, *Early Greek Philosophy* (Presocratics) (Harmondsworth, 1987).
R. K. Sprague, *The Older Sophists: A Complete Translation* (Columbia, South Carolina, 1972).

(A widely-available translation of the evidence for the sophists with introduction and notes would be a useful addition to our resources.)

Kirk, Raven, Schofield, *Presocratic Philosophers*, and Wright, *Presocratics*, contain bibliographies. For the sophists, see G. B. Kerferd, *The Sophistic Movement* (Cambridge, 1981).

Socrates and Plato:
G. Vlastos, *Socrates: Ironist and Moral Philosopher* (Cambridge, 1991), is a major study with full bibliography; Vlastos, *Socratic Studies*, ed. M. Burnyeat (Cambridge, 1994), contains the final version of some of Vlastos's key articles on Socratic method.
On the subjects treated in this book, J. Annas, *An Introduction to Plato's*

Republic (Oxford, 1981), and T. Irwin, *Plato's Ethics* (Oxford, 1995) are most useful. See also R. Kraut, ed., *The Cambridge Companion to Plato* (Cambridge, 1992). For good philosophical reasons, it is difficult to offer an overall account of Plato's theories; C. J. Rowe, *Plato* (Brighton , 1984) explores some themes lucidly.

The most recent Penguin Classics, The World's Classics, and Hackett translations, as well as the Oxford Clarendon Plato Series, have good introductions, notes, and bibliographies (also the standard Stephanus page numbers and letters); Plato is best studied dialogue by dialogue, and so these translations represent the best starting-point. Aris & Phillips (Warminster) have recently published several dialogues, with text, translation, and commentary: these include *Meno*, ed. R. W. Sharples (1985), *Republic V* , ed. S. Halliwell (1993), and *Statesman*, ed. C. J. Rowe (1995). (See further the useful survey of recent work on Plato by C. J. Rowe in *Phronesis* 39 (1994), 214–24.)

Aristotle:
In translations of Aristotle, it is highly desirable to be able to correlate the translation with the standard Bekker page nos. and lines of the Greek text. This can be done with J. Barnes, ed., *The Complete Works of Aristotle: The Revised Oxford Translation*, 2 vols. (Princeton, 1984), J. Ackrill, ed., *A New Aristotle Reader* (selections) (Oxford, 1987), and the Oxford Clarendon Aristotle Series. The most recent Penguin Classics (e.g. T. J. Saunders's revision of T. A. Sinclair's tr. of *Politics* (Harmondsworth, 1981), and The World's Classics (e.g. R. F. Stalley's revision of E. Barker's tr. of *Politics*)) provide the Bekker numbering section by section. On the areas covered in this book, especially useful works on ethics are: A. O. Rorty, ed., *Essays on Aristotle's* Ethics (Oxford, 1980); R. Kraut, *Aristotle on the Human Good* (Princeton, 1989); on politics, D. Keyt and F. Miller, edd., *A Companion to Aristotle's* Politics (Oxford, 1991); G. Patzig, ed., *Aristoteles Politik* (Göttingen, 1990). See also J. Lear, *Aristotle: the Desire to Understand* (Cambridge, 1988); T. Irwin, *Aristotle's First Principles* (Oxford, 1988).

Hellenistic Philosophy:
A. A. Long and D. N. Sedley, *The Hellenistic Philosophers* (Cambridge, 1987), vol. 1, translations and commentary, vol. 2, texts, notes, and bibliography provide the essential basis. B. Inwood and L. P. Gerson, tr. *Hellenistic Philosophy: Introductory Readings* (Indianapolis, 1988) give longer extracts.
Several first-rate volumes give a good picture of recent work:

M. Schofield, M. Burnyeat, J. Barnes, edd., *Doubt and Dogmatism: Studies in Hellenistic Epistemology* (Oxford, 1980).

J. Barnes, J. Brunschwig, M. Burnyeat, M. Schofield, edd., *Science and Speculations; Studies in Hellenistic Theory and Practice* (Cambridge/Paris, 1982).

M. Schofield and G. Striker, edd., *The Norms of Nature: Studies in Hellenistic Ethics* (Cambridge/Paris, 1986).

H. Flashar and O. Gigon, edd., *Aspects de la philosophie hellénistique*, Fondation Hardt, *Entretiens sur l'antiquité classique* 32 (Vandoeuvres-Geneva, 1986).

J. Brunschwig and M. C. Nussbaum, edd., *Passions and Perceptions: Studies in the Hellenistic Philosophy of Mind* (Cambridge/Paris, 1993).

A. Laks and M. Schofield, edd., *Justice and Generosity: Studies in Hellenistic Social and Political Philosophy* (Cambridge/Paris, 1995).

Note also J. Annas, *Hellenistic Philosophy of Mind* (Berkeley, 1992); B. Inwood, *Ethics and Human Action in Early Stoicism* (Oxford, 1985); P. Mitsis, *Epicurus' Ethical Theory: The Pleasures of Invulnerability* (Ithaca, 1988); M. C. Nussbaum, *The Therapy of Desire: Theory and Practice in Hellenistic Ethics* (Princeton, 1994); and M. Schofield, *The Stoic Idea of the City* (Cambridge, 1991).

ABOUT THE AUTHOR

Christopher Gill b. 1946 has held teaching appointments in Classics at the Universities of Yale and Bristol, and the University of Wales, Aberystwyth; he held a one-year research fellowship at the National Humanities Center, North Carolina, USA. He is presently Reader in Ancient Thought at the University of Exeter. He has published many articles and book-chapters on Greek and Roman philosophy and literature. His publications include: *Plato: The Atlantis Story*, Plato's texts on Atlantis with introduction and commentary (Bristol, 1980); (ed.) *The Person and the Human Mind: Issues in Ancient and Modern Philosophy* (Oxford, 1990); (ed., with T. P. Wiseman) *Lies and Fiction in the Ancient World* (Exeter and Texas, 1993). Forthcoming publications include: *Personality in Greek Epic, Tragedy, and Philosophy: The Self in Dialogue* (Oxford); (ed., with M. M. McCabe) *Form and Argument in Late Plato* (Oxford); (ed., with S. Braund) *The Passions in Roman Thought and Literature* (Cambridge); (ed., with N. Postlethwaite and R. Seaford) *Reciprocity in Ancient Greece* (Oxford).

INDEX OF NAMES, SUBJECTS, AND PASSAGES